WHISPERING
IN GOD'S EAR

TRUE STORIES INSPIRING CHILDLIKE FAITH

FEATURING STORIES BY

BETH MOORE

KAY ARTHUR

EUGENE PETERSON

GIGI GRAHAM

AND OTHERS

COMPILED BY **WAYNE HOLMES**

WATERBROOK
PRESS

WHISPERING IN GOD'S EAR
PUBLISHED BY WATERBROOK PRESS
2375 Telstar Drive, Suite 160
Colorado Springs, Colorado 80920
A division of Random House, Inc.

Other permissions and acknowledgments appear on pages 255–262.

ISBN 1-57856-899-4

Library of Congress Cataloging-in-Publication Data
  Whispering in God's Ear : true stories inspiring childlike faith / compiled by Wayne Holmes.—1st ed.
    p. cm.
  Includes bibliographical references and index.
  ISBN 1-57856-899-4 (alk. paper)
  1. Prayer—Christianity—Miscellanea. I. Wayne Holmes.
BV213.C38 2005
242—dc22   2005007774

Printed in the United States of America
2005—First Edition

10 9 8 7 6 5 4 3 2 1

—◄o►—◄o►—

Dedicated to my children—
Brett, Melissa, Barcley, and Crystal

CONTENTS

Acknowledgments ix

Introduction 1

PART ONE: "PLEASE LET ME SEE A FROG"
Children Praying

Five Is Not Too Young by Corrie ten Boom 5

Plum Purple City Lights by Janet Lynn Mitchell 9

A Mother's Day Prayer by Stacy Rothenberger 11

A Son's Prayer by Martha Rogers 14

Nikes and Mustard Seeds by Susanna Flory 18

I Lift Up My Eyes to the Hills by Jeanne Zornes 21

A Simple Prayer by Kathryn Lay 24

PART TWO: "HELP ME NOT LIKE MY ANIMALS"
Children Leading

Shirley's Story by Gloria Gaither and Shirley Dobson 29

Faith in God's Living Word by Sally Clarkson 34

Smokin' Joe by Barb Eimer 38

A Little Boy's Prayer by Janet Sketchley 41

Listening Prayers by Jennifer A. Schuchmann 44

Of Teddy Bears and Missionaries by Sharon Hinck 47

PART THREE: "WHEN I GROW UP"
Children Playing

Divine Interruptions by Patty Stump 54

"When I Grow Up" by Robert Benson 57

"Sewing" Seeds of Faith by Joy Brown 60

God Is With Us by Peggy Morris 63

Wee-Ones Worship by Kelly Hayes 65

Emma's Place by Jennifer A. Schuchmann 67

PART FOUR: "I FOUND IT"
Children Believing

The Lost Contact by Kay Arthur 75

Called to Deliver Others by Heather Whitestone McCallum
    and Angela Hunt 78

Looking for T. T. by Linda Knight 80

Pastry Bag Faith by Pat Butler 83

Praying for Snow by C. Ellen Watts 86

The Trivial Prayer by JoAnn Reno Wray 89

Potato Chip Prayers by Jean Hall 92

PART FIVE: "I HAVE HEARD HIS VOICE"
Children Trusting

Fanny Crosby by Ethel Barrett 99

Bicycle Prayers by Ruth Bell Graham 105

Childhood Years by Kathleen White 107

Words Worth Remembering by Patty Stump 109

"God Cut Me" by Karen Tenney Hitchcock 113

Jumping in the Deep End by Patrick Borders 116

PART SIX: "DEAR JESUS, WE NEED A DADDY"
Children Asking

Bibles, Baptism, Certificates, and Other Signs of Church Life
by Beth Moore 121

Innocent Petitions by Robin Jones Gunn 124

The Problem by Gigi Graham 126

Wanted: A Friend by Lynn Schwander 128

"We Need a Daddy" by Marilyn Martyn McAuley 131

Kelsey's Prayer by Lanita Bradley Boyd 134

Trey's Prayer by Dorothy Hill 137

PART SEVEN: "DO I HAF TO TELL YOU WHAT I DONE?"
Children Praying Honestly

Disowned Desire by John Eldredge 144

The Day Bart Simpson Prayed by Lee Strobel 146

The Flat Tire by Tony Campolo 150

A Double Dose of Lessons by Laurie Barker Copeland 153

A Loving Reminder by Anita Higman 155

An Honest Heart by Diane H. Pitts 157

PART EIGHT: "WOULD YOU PLEASE HEAL MY GRANDPA?"
Children Persisting

One Ring by Phil Callaway 164

Black Shoes and Christmas by Cecil Murphey 167

"Dear God, It's Me, Nathaniel" by Elizabeth M. Thompson 173

Consider the Daffodils by Heidi VanderSlikke 177

Hamster Prayers by Donita K. Paul 181

The Unfailing Faith of a Praying Child by Brenda R. Coats 184

PART NINE: "WOW, GOD!"
Children Thanking

Pão, Senhor? by Max Lucado 189

Bedtime Rituals by Lori Borgman 191

Disabled Dreams by Tamara Boggs 194

The Day the Sandman Came by Gigi Graham 197

Just Say "Wow!" by Barbara Eubanks 200

A Holy Presence by Lois Pecce 202

PART TEN: "IN THE NAME OF JESUS"
Children Healing

The Laying On of Hands by Richard J. Foster 207

"It's Okay, Mommy" by Michelle Medlock Adams 209

One Child's Prayer by Patricia Stebelton 213

Simple Faith by Lisa Eblen Wiener 218

A Prayer of Faith by Diana J. Baker 220

A Brother's Gift by Emily Sue Harvey 222

PART ELEVEN: "OPEN ARMS AND SLOBBERY KISSES"
Children Loving

Communion by Eugene H. Peterson 229

Telling the Truth by Sheila Walsh 231

The God Who Gives Back by Bruce Wilkinson 233

Annie's Prayer by Jean Davis 236

Little Signs of Love by Sharon Hinck 240

A Mark of Grace by H. Michael Brewer 244

Author Profiles 246

Credits and Permissions 255

ACKNOWLEDGMENTS

I am grateful to my children, Crystal, Barcley, Melissa, and Brett, for the lessons they have taught me. Some I have learned with ease; some I have learned with great reluctance. Other lessons they have tried to teach me I am still learning. There have been many wonderful times in our lives as well as some difficult ones. Through it all I have felt God's love in differing ways. I wish I could give back to them as much as they have given to me, but they will have to experience for themselves the joy—and sorrows—of being a parent.

My wife, Linda, deserves an extra measure of thanks for her loving support. This work could not have been accomplished had she not given so selflessly.

Special appreciation goes to my agent, Karen Solem, and her helper, Maria.

To Elisa Stanford and the team at WaterBrook Press—thanks for your hard work and faith in this endeavor.

Special thanks to Cecil (Cec) Murphey who graciously helped with the edits and who has been a true friend extraordinaire.

I also want to thank Mike Brewer, Joe Lacy, and Dan Edelen who have added their insights to my writing endeavors.

Special thanks to the parents who shared the prayers of their children. These added a special touch: a smile, a laugh, and occasionally a tear or two.

To all the writers and friends who have supported this book—some by contributing stories; others by their prayers—I am indebted to you.

Finally, to the children who have shared their stories and prayers—thank you. You are an inspiration and teachers of God's wisdom.

INTRODUCTION

D addy, Daddy, come look," Crystal squealed with excitement. She was at the age where coming home from work was pure joy for me because of the hugs and kisses she so freely gave. On this day she didn't stop for affection. Instead she rushed around the corner and headed for her room, confident that I would follow.

As I came around the corner and entered her world, I saw her pull a musical instrument out of a case. "Look, Daddy," she said as she proudly held up a violin and bow for my inspection. "Isn't it neat?" She raised the violin and placed it under her chin. She then took the bow and pulled it across the strings, making a most unpleasant sound. Back and forth the bow ran across the strings. I made a concerted effort not to wince.

"Isn't it great? I just got it today, and they said I could keep it."

"That's wonderful, honey."

Though the sound was uninviting, the spirited performance was precious. Elation shone in her eyes and in her heart.

Crystal's musical career faded a few months later. Like many young children, she lost interest in the instrument and found other activities to fill her days. But I will never forget the excitement and wonder of that moment. I witnessed pure joy—the kind of joy I had not experienced for quite some time—and I was deeply touched by the sound of ecstasy that flowed from her heart.

I could have reacted with indifference. I could have allowed the unpleasantness of the sound to spoil the moment. Fortunately, I listened with my heart and heard the spirit that outplayed the instrument—and I was cautious not to crush her creativity.

As a child, and occasionally as an adult, I have experienced the joy and excitement of a new endeavor. Just as Crystal wanted to share with her daddy, I also want to share things with my heavenly Father. I am reminded that I can bring anything to Him in prayer, and He will listen—without wincing—no matter how it sounds to His ears. He is a more loving Father than I could ever hope to be, and He is always careful with His children—cautious never to crush their spirits or quell their creativity.

Nowhere is God's listening ear more keen than when it comes to kids and prayer. When children pray, they open up their hearts to the One who knows them best, loves them the most, and accepts them unreservedly. Kids love from their hearts. That is, they believe without doubt, trust without reservation, live without reluctance, sleep without worry, and laugh without restraint.

I miss the simple faith that trusts so readily and lives so simply. But, if we will listen to the prayers of our children, we just might learn to recapture some of the laughter and love that was once so commonplace in our own lives. *Whispering in God's Ear: True Stories Inspiring Childlike Faith* is a collection of stories about prayer that reveal spiritual truths through the eyes of children. In selecting and preparing the stories for this book, I discovered a simple, childlike faith that led me into a deeper prayer relationship with God. My prayer is that you will once again see the world through eyes of hope, love, and wonder.

—*Wayne*

PART ONE

"PLEASE LET ME SEE A FROG"

Children Praying

Dear God. It is about time! It sure has been ugly since the leaves fell. But are You going to be mad at someone for spilling all of that glitter?

—SAVANNAH, age four, after a walk with her mother through snow-covered woods

Help my mom and dad stop fighting, and help my brother to be nicer to me so they can all go to heaven with me.

—DANA, age four

God, I am having trouble sleeping! It sure would help if you would turn down that sun's volume!

—CAMERON, age four and having trouble falling asleep for his nap

No matter how bad life tastes, prayer makes it sweeter.

—ASHTYN, age six

C hildren praying. What instantly spring to my mind are images of kids kneeling beside their beds, heads bowed, eyes closed (sometimes), while parents and angels watch. Children's petitions are as varied as the kids who offer them.

Some children pray for personal things, such as passing a science test, seeing a frog, or defeating the class bully.

Some pray for pressing needs, such as the healing of a parent, food for the table, or a father for the family.

Some offer prayers of thanks: for the sunshine, for a mother's love, or for their country.

Some of my favorite prayers are for assistance: Help Mom not to be grumpy; help me not to be angry; help my dad not to be upset with me when he finds out what I did.

The petitioners have at least one thing in common: All are doing business with the God of the universe.

The lessons we learn from our kids' prayers aren't necessarily profound. Usually they are basic ones. But we need a reminder that the basic lessons—God loves us, God hears us, and God answers prayer—are the ones we need to revisit.

—*Wayne*

FIVE IS NOT TOO YOUNG

Corrie ten Boom

from *In My Father's House*

In 1892, the year I was born, Holland was entering an exciting and important era. In a few years, Wilhelmina would be crowned Queen at the tender age of eighteen. There were signs which indicated that the stability of that latter part of the nineteenth century would soon be rocked by the rattling of German swords. Foreign policy was being shaped around lines of power, as young Kaiser Wilhelm II ruled the country which later played such an important part in my life.

History in the making means nothing to a child, but it was a world event for me when Mother or Tante Anna pinched a guilder hard enough to squeeze out some sugar and butter for those fat little sugar cookies I loved. The fragrance of baking would float from the iron stove into the shop, and tantalize the customers just as it put us in a happy mood.

When I was five years old, I learned to read; I loved stories, particularly those about Jesus. He was a member of the ten Boom family—it was just as easy to talk to Him as it was to carry on a conversation with my mother and father, my aunts, or my brother and sisters. He was there.

One day my mother was watching me play house. In my little girl world of fantasy, she saw that I was pretending to call on a neighbor. I knocked on the make-believe door and waited...no one answered.

"Corrie, I know Someone who is standing at your door and knocking right now."

Was she playing a game with me? I know now that there was a preparation within my childish heart for that moment; the Holy Spirit makes us ready for acceptance of Jesus Christ, of turning our life over to Him.

"Jesus said that He is standing at the door, and if you invite Him in He will come into your heart," my mother continued. "Would you like to invite Jesus in?"

At that moment my mother was the most beautiful person in the whole world to me.

"Yes, Mama, I want Jesus in my heart."

So she took my little hand in hers and we prayed together. It was so simple, and yet Jesus Christ says that we all must come as children, no matter what our age, social standing, or intellectual background.

When Mother told me later about this experience, I recalled it clearly.

BUT, YOU'RE SO LITTLE

Does a child of five really know what he's doing? Some people say that children don't have spiritual understanding—that we should wait until a child can "make up his mind for himself." I believe a child should be led, not left to wander.

Jesus became more real to me from that time on. Mother told me later that I began to pray for others, as young as I was.

The street behind our house was the Smedestraat. It was filled with saloons, and many of the happenings there were frightening to me. As I played outside jumping rope, or joined with Nollie, my sister, in a game of *bikkelen* (ball and stones), I saw the police pick up these lurching, incoherent men as they slumped to the ground or slouched in a doorway, and take them into the police station.

I would stand before the *politie bureau* (police station) behind the

Beje, and watch the drunks being pushed in. It made me shiver. The building was made of dark red brick, and 'way at the top were turrets with small windows. Were those the cells, I wondered?

It was in that same police station years later that my father, and all his children, and a grandson were taken after being arrested for helping Jews escape from the German gestapo.

As a child I would be so concerned for those arrested that I would run into the house sobbing, "Mother...I'm afraid those poor men are going to be hurt...they're so sick!"

Bless Mother's understanding. She would say, "Pray for them, Corrie."

And I would pray for the drunks. "Dear Jesus, please help those men...and Jesus, help all the people on the Smedestraat."

Many years later I spoke on a television station in Holland. I received a letter after the program which said: "My husband was especially interested because you told us that you had lived in Haarlem. He lived in a house on the Smedestraat. Three years ago he accepted the Lord Jesus as his Savior."

I read that letter and recalled the prayers of little Corrie. That man whose wife wrote me was one person I had prayed for seventy-six years before.

DOES HE LISTEN?

At another time in my later years I was camping with a number of Haarlem girls. Around the campfire one evening, we were talking about the Lord and chatting about the pleasant events of the day.

"Do you know that I am a neighbor of yours?" one of the girls asked me. "I live in the Smedestraat."

"I lived there until five years ago," said another girl.

"My mother lived there," said a third.

We all began to laugh to discover that all eighteen of those girls, who were sleeping in the big camp tent, had lived on that street or their parents had lived there. They found it an amusing coincidence.

"Listen," I said, "I just remembered something that I had almost forgotten. When I was five or six years old, I used to pray every day for the people in the Smedestraat. The fact that we have been talking about Jesus, and that God has even used me to reach some of your parents, is an answer to the prayer of a little child. Never doubt whether God hears our prayers, even the unusual ones."

How often we think when a prayer is not answered that God has said *no*. Many times He has simply said, *"Wait."*

Plum Purple City Lights

Janet Lynn Mitchell

M om, I've found exactly what I want for Christmas! It will look great in my room!"

Wanting to buy my daughter what she truly desired, I went to the store to buy Jenna's 2000 Christmas present—a thirteen-foot wallpaper mural of Manhattan's skyline. In just weeks my sixteen-year-old daughter's bedroom took on a new look. The night lights of the Manhattan Bridge, the Empire State Building, and the Twin Towers stretched across her wall. Curtains, a bedspread, and a lamp were the added touches to convert Jenna's California hideaway into the glittering lights of New York City.

Truthfully, I did not share Jenna's taste in interior design. We had spent hours together shopping and contemplating different ways she could redecorate her room. I'd shown her flowers in pinks and yellows, and she again escorted me back to the store to take "one more look" at lower Manhattan at dusk, fashioned in plum purple and blues.

"It's cool. I love it! Can't you see? The city is alive, and its lights reflect a silhouette of the New York skyline on the water. Look. There are even two American flags flying."

I saw them. The two American flags were the size of small safety pins. To me, the mural reflected a busy city, full of action and little peace. But nevertheless, this was for *Jenna's* room.

Like many moms, each night since Jenna was born, I've eased my way into my daughter's room. I ask Jenna about her day and listen to her dreams for the future. I've also sat waiting patiently for the results of her last blood test of the day—praying that her blood-sugar levels would be in the safety range for her to go to sleep, and then determining how much insulin she would need to get her through the night.

During our moments of managing her diabetes, we've often studied the skyline on her wall, pointing out different places we want to visit someday. Night after night Jenna and I surveyed different buildings and skyscrapers, pondering what their occupants might have done that day. I often pointed to the Twin Towers, sometimes even laying my hand across them saying, "Let's pray for the people who work there."

Jenna always responded, "I pray for them every night."

Life in New York City drastically changed after September 11, 2001, and so has the skyline. But Jenna's room remains unchanged. The Twin Towers still stand tall, attached to Jenna's wall. Those two little flags the size of safety pins remain—untouched—declaring our freedom.

I now see what wasn't clear when I purchased the wallpaper mural. It's more than okay for moms and daughters to differ in their likes. God gave Jenna her taste of interior design and her desire for a wall mural of Manhattan. And for an entire year, despite Jenna's own need for a healing touch from God, she prayed for people she didn't know and for a city she'd never seen.

◄o►◄o►

I still find my way to Jenna's room each night. She tests her blood as we talk about her day and her plans for tomorrow. Just before I kiss her good night, a lump forms in my throat. I try to speak as I point toward Jenna's wall mural.

"I know, Mom," she whispers while gazing at her wall. "I'm still praying."

A Mother's Day Prayer

Stacy Rothenberger

Reviewing the events of our day is something our kids expect as part of their nightly routine.

One night we were discussing an event that had happened that day at the mall. While trying on shoes, we had come across a cantankerous little girl. The first words out of her mouth were "I'm bigger than you." She was speaking to my four-year-old daughter, Danielle, who was obviously a foot taller than she. I smiled one of those "Oh, aren't you cute" smiles and turned away thinking that if we ignored her, she would just go away. No such luck.

"You're dumb."

Okay, now she was talking about my baby. Before Danielle could fire back a mean comment, I pulled her aside and suggested we ignore the little girl without retaliating. This proved to be quite a task because that kid wasn't content with bad-mouthing Danielle, she also attacked my six-year-old son, Dalton.

"I don't like you. You're stupid."

Before I lost it, the child's mother intervened. "Samantha, you shouldn't talk to people like that."

Fortunately, they left before anyone could bring out the gloves.

That night Danielle was still upset by what had happened at the shoe store. "The next time I see Samantha I'm going to tell her to stop being so mean," she said.

I suggested that maybe Samantha had been having a bad day. Maybe there was something upsetting her, and the best thing we could do for her was to pray for her. So we did.

Danielle folded her hands, bowed her head, and in an angelic voice, whispered, "Dear Lord, please help Samantha not be so grumpy. Help her have a happy heart that is full of Jesus. Amen."

We were sharing a precious moment. Unfortunately, reality happened. After her prayer Danielle decided to run downstairs and kiss her daddy good night. As the kids were calling out their final good-nights, they woke ten-month-old Drew, whose crib is at the top of the stairs.

"Guys, be quiet! You just woke up Drew! Go to bed!" I stomped to my bedroom, fuming because they had messed up my schedule. (Instead of reading my new parenting book, I had to take care of Drew.)

Then I heard the patter of little feet. That made me angrier because it meant that someone was out of bed. I saw Dalton's impish face peeking in at my door.

"Mom, can I pray for you?"

"Of course, you can pray for me," I said as I felt the tension release from my mind and body.

I gave Dalton a hug and a kiss and watched as he returned to his room to pray for me. About five minutes later I heard Dalton return. This time I didn't have the anger I normally would have had when a child was out of bed.

"Mom, I just wanted to let you know that I prayed for you." Those words came from a kid who has never enjoyed praying aloud.

"What did you pray for?"

"I prayed that God would take away your grumpiness, that you would have a good night, and that you would have a great Mother's Day tomorrow."

I thanked him and assured him that God had already answered his prayer. Dalton had given me the best Mother's Day present.

◄○►◄○►

The simple prayers of my children reminded me that God cares about everything in my life. Nothing is too trivial for Him to handle. When someone hurts my feelings by careless words, I can go to God in prayer. When my life is interrupted and things don't work out according to my schedule, I can take it to my heavenly Father. He responds to my child-like faith by bringing a smile to my lips and comfort to my life.

A SON'S PRAYER

Martha Rogers

M others aren't supposed to play favorites, and I don't. Each of our boys has a special place in my heart, but Mike, the youngest, and I have a closer relationship than I enjoyed with my older two sons. His delightful personality and corny sense of humor have cheered me up on more than one occasion. When Mike came along, both brothers were in school, and I could spend more time alone with him. I took the year off from teaching to stay at home during his first year.

One summer in particular stands out in my mind and fills my heart with love and gratitude for Mike's strong faith. Mike graduated from college, became engaged to a girl he met there, and landed a great job to begin in the fall. He came home to live with us until his wedding, which was to be on January 2.

For the first time in twenty-eight years I would not be returning to my high-school classroom that fall. My contract had not been renewed at the private school where I had taught for the past ten years. A difference in opinion with the headmaster resulted in my termination. My self-esteem fell to an all-time low. I moped around and felt miserable as well as angry toward the parents who caused the situation and the board members who supported them instead of me.

Mike spent the summer cheering me up and trying to take my mind off the approaching fall semester. His fiancée lived in Dallas, and he made trips to see her on the weekends, but during the week we spent time together. His oddball jokes served as just the medicine I needed.

I began looking on the bright side of the situation—I didn't have to spend long days preparing lesson plans and updating files for school. I attended a special week of noonday services with Mike at our church during the normal week of in-service at school.

Mike took me to lunch on several occasions, and I helped him select a wardrobe befitting a young businessman. At one particular store, he entered the dressing room, arms laden with suits, slacks, and jackets. I sat outside the area and waited for him to reappear. He put on quite a fashion show, and I laughed until I cried at some of the zany combinations he pulled together. How about a green and white stripe shirt with a black-and-white-check jacket, brown slacks, and purple tie?

His final purchases, though, were more in keeping with his position as an accountant for a well-known firm. He even talked me into buying a few things for myself. The closeness we developed brought me joy at a time when I greatly needed it. Although my anger and resentment toward the school board remained, my time with Mike pushed it out of my mind.

The week before Mike was to begin his job, we made a few last trips to the mall for shirts, ties, and other accessories. Loaded down with shopping bags, we decided to stop for lunch in the food court.

After paying for our food selections, we meandered toward a table overlooking the ice-skating rink in the center of the mall. We made small talk and commented on the skaters gliding across the ice below us. I noticed that Mike seemed nervous about something, but I attributed it to the jitters about beginning a new job.

Finally, when I could no longer ignore the fidgeting and napkin shredding, I shoved my empty plate aside and leaned my elbows on the table. "Okay, out with it. What's bothering you? Your job? The wedding?"

Mike averted his gaze and worked his mouth in that funny little way he did when he had something to say that he didn't want to say. I waited patiently for him to either share or decide it was time to leave.

After a few minutes, he turned to face me. "I have a confession to make, and I hope you won't be mad at me."

I frowned. My mind raced with ideas. He'd broken up with Sloane. He didn't have a job. "Mad at you?"

He twiddled a plastic fork with his fingers. "Yes." He shrugged his shoulders. "Remember last spring when I was home on break?"

Yes, I did remember. Our break times did not coincide, and I was so involved with grading tests, averaging grades, and getting report cards ready, I hadn't been able to spend any time with him. In fact, my late-night work on the computer and printer in the room next to his kept him awake—something he mentioned several times.

I nodded. "We didn't do the things we'd talked about doing, did we?"

"No, you were too busy with school stuff. You were tired all the time too. How could you stay up so late and still go to work the next day?"

"Well, I was used to it. Did it all the time." I shook my head. "But that's not your confession. What's really going on?"

He grinned. "It's not really so bad. I just didn't expect the results to be what they were."

"Okay, now you're making me nervous. What did you do?"

"Well, I kept thinking about how tired you were and how tied up with schoolwork you were. I prayed for God to somehow get you out from under the load." Then he took my hand in his. "I didn't mean to pray you out of a job."

I sat in stunned silence, and the anger and resentment I had stored up for the past few months disappeared. Peace and calm filled the space. "I'm not angry with you for that. You love me enough to pray for me, and that's a blessing. God must have something great in store for me this year to answer your prayer in such a way."

His lopsided grin brought a smile to my heart. No matter what came my way in the next few months, nothing would surpass knowing that my son loved me enough to pray for my load to be lighter.

Looking back I realize that the only way God could get me out of spending more time with students and grades than I did with my own family was to hit me with the termination.

A son's prayer offered for a tired mother opened up the opportunity for God to begin a new work in my life. I went on to teach eight years at the college level and to pursue a writing career I never would have had otherwise.

NIKES AND MUSTARD SEEDS

Susanna Flory

They were Nike baby shoes. Little, white leather athletic shoes with a sky blue "swoosh" on the sides.

The cost? Forty-seven dollars. I really couldn't afford the shoes, but I bought them anyway, which made them more precious. I cleaned them. I polished them. I loved those little Nike shoes.

One day my kids and I decided to go on a hike. My son was five. My daughter couldn't walk well yet, so I carried her in a backpack. I laced the prized Nike shoes tightly onto her squirmy, soft feet, and we set off on a beautiful fall day, taking a hilly trail through a grove of oak trees. We hiked up and down, and my daughter laughed and pointed her fat little fingers at the birds and butterflies as she bounced along in the backpack. My legs strained as we climbed the steep, hilly trails, and the air grew warmer as we passed through bright breaks in the forest.

Finally we came to the trail's end, sweating, tired, and ready for a break. As I stood in the shade, taking a few deep breaths, I felt my daughter's little, squirmy foot rub along my back. That felt strange. It was soft. Too soft. I looked down, and my heart gave a jolt. I saw a little pink leg, a soft, white sock. No shoe.

I turned around, craning my head from side to side, frantically scanning the ground around and past us on up the trail. Nothing. The dirt was a dusty red, so the polished white shoe would easily stand out. I should be able to see it, but I couldn't. I began to breathe a little harder. What if I couldn't find it?

I took a few hesitant steps up the trail as my daughter joyfully kicked. She thought we were continuing our hike. Feeling distinctly joyless, I felt my throat tighten and my chest hurt as I realized how difficult it would be to find her shoe if she had kicked it off into the thick ivy that wound along the sides of the trail.

My mind took off in endless whirls, a new worry with each heavy step. *What if I can't find the shoe? I love those shoes! There's no way I can afford to buy new ones. What will my husband say?*

Then I stopped. Stood. Fretted.

That's when five-year-old Ethan spoke. His clear, earnest gaze smoothed away my frown. "Mommy, why don't you pray?"

That was it. So simple.

Ethan and I held hands and prayed together in the woods: "God, we lost Thea's shoe. We can't find it anywhere. We don't know what to do. Please help us."

If my son's faith was a mustard seed, then mine was a dust mite. I said the words, but I didn't trust. Ethan did. We grownups play at faith while children practice it.

Besides being practical, Ethan's faith was also immediate. A friend once told me he was asking God for "now" faith. The phrase caught my attention; I didn't recall ever seeing "now" faith in the Bible. Smiling, he'd read Hebrews 11:1 to me: "*Now* faith is being sure of what we hope for and certain of what we do not see" (emphasis added). If we live by faith, we must be ready to act on it. God calls us to immediate, ready-for-battle, "now" faith.

Back in the woods, I didn't have "now" faith. After Ethan and I prayed, I opened my eyes, outwardly calm but with worry hiding underneath the surface of my emotions like an oily river tainted with unbelief and cynicism.

Then, in the dark of the woods, I saw something. Fifty yards away, a column of light broke through the trees—a ray of sunshine that penetrated the tangled branches of the old oak forest. The ray gleamed, transfiguring the slowly rising dust into particles of floating gold. It was so bright that the surrounding forest grew even darker.

But it was what the dazzling ray of sunlight illuminated that caught my eye. The lost shoe. It lay on its side in the red dust, gleaming, the center of a golden circle.

I was speechless, at once amazed at the miracle and ashamed of my doubts. I ran toward the precious shoe, my heart full. My five-year-old wasn't fazed. He of the towering faith thought it was no big deal. It was as if he knew the shoe would be there, lying on the red dirt, cradled in a circle of light.

I needed to know, that day, the smallness of my faith. I needed to see "now" faith in action. I needed a miracle that day, and I got one, thanks to Ethan.

I Lift Up My Eyes to the Hills

Jeanne Zornes

he heart-stopping *bam!* beneath my side of the car meant my fears had come true.

"Flat tire!" my dad grumbled as he wrestled the steering wheel of our limping car. As he brought it to a stop at the edge of the narrow mountain road, I looked out my passenger window and panicked. Below us yawned a deep chasm.

"Everybody out on the driver's side," my dad demanded. Mom slid across the front seat as my sister and I, shaking, slid across the back. Any second I expected our car to go tumbling down the side of the mountain.

I was eight years old, anticipating a fun family vacation. My mother wanted to see her cousins who lived in a remote little town in southern Washington, right above the Columbia River. We could have gotten there by taking a highway down to Oregon, then east to a ferry. Or, as Mother suggested, we could take some back roads that wound through Washington's Cascade Mountains.

Even though the map showed just two thin lines for part of the route—meaning "primitive road"—Dad felt we could do it. At first ascending into the mountains was fun. Our old blue and white Oldsmobile kicked up dust behind it as the gravel road snaked higher and higher. Trees spiked to the sky, seeming to snag the cottony clouds overhead.

But after a while, all the curves made me feel nauseated. We'd closed our windows because of the dust, and the stuffy air in the car made me feel sicker. I didn't like how Dad drove close to the right-hand side of the narrow road, next to the drop-offs.

"Don't drive so close to the edge," I pleaded.

"I can't drive in the middle," he replied. "Some car might come around the next corner. We'd have a crash."

But we hadn't seen another car for miles.

Then came the flat tire, with our car stopped precariously in the soft gravel.

My mother and teenage sister scrambled for big rocks to secure the other tires, while my dad lifted luggage out of the trunk.

"Get over by the hillside," my dad told me. He wanted me out of danger. And I was too scared to be of much help anyway.

What could I possibly do? I watched my sister and mother frantically dig out trenches for the tires with flat rocks. Dad tried to jack up the car, but it began sliding down the soft shoulder. Quickly he released the jack.

And while all this happened, I prayed. I prayed like I never had before. Until now I'd considered prayer something you did at mealtime and bedtime. Oh yes, I also prayed certain times at church. But would God care about what was happening to our family on a remote road in the mountains?

"O God, help us," I managed through sobs. "Send somebody to help us."

Within minutes another car came from the opposite direction. Then another arrived behind us. The men devised a plan to save our slipping car and helped Dad change the tire. Then we went on our way, finally reaching a paved road and our cousins' tiny town.

That trip changed my child's perception of prayer. I realized I could pray to God anywhere, anytime, for anything. God wasn't too busy to hear a child's prayers, even when they came from a lonely road in the mountains.

Later I learned that a psalmist experienced something similar:

I lift up my eyes to the hills—
    where does my help come from?
My help comes from the LORD,
    the Maker of heaven and earth. (Psalm 121:1-2)

A SIMPLE PRAYER

Kathryn Lay

P lease let me see a frog tonight, in Jesus's name, amen."

I gave a good-night hug to Michelle, my four-year-old daughter, and tucked her into bed with her favorite books to look at. We had been talking about frogs and lizards and turtles that day, three of her favorite creatures.

"When will the frog come?" she asked.

I smiled. "Well, I haven't seen any frogs yet this year; we'll just have to wait and see." I felt bad that she would be disappointed.

"God can do anything," she announced. "Just like my daddy."

A lump filled my throat. She trusted in her father *and* her heavenly Father. Difficult times had made me wonder if God still answered prayers.

I went into the kitchen to do the dishes. With my hands immersed in hot, soapy water, I closed my eyes. *I know it's a silly request, God. But there's something about the way she truly believes that You'll answer her prayer. Do you hear her? Do you hear me?*

Later my husband returned home from his volunteer job at church teaching English as a Second Language classes for refugees. Michelle had been asleep an hour.

Richard and I talked over our day and how the classes had gone that night.

"Oops, laundry," I said, jumping up to move the wet clothes from the washer to the dryer. I turned on the garage light, startled by movement near the open door that led to the backyard.

Our dog barked at the corner of the garage, stopping to sniff at something.

I took a careful step forward, ready to run if one of our giant, fast-moving water bugs should suddenly head my way.

Near the back door sat a large, bug-eyed, brown frog.

"Outside," I ordered the dog, who reluctantly padded to the backyard.

After a momentary chase, with the frog two hops ahead, I held the bulging, squirming creature in my hands and carried my prize into the house. "Hey, look," I said, holding the frog out to my husband. "I think Tippy was about to have a late-night snack of frog legs."

"Wow, it's too bad Michelle's not awake," he said.

My mouth dropped open when I remembered her prayer.

"Quick," I said, "Follow me."

My surprised husband stared at me as if I'd done one too many loads of laundry. He followed me down the hall to Michelle's room. I held the frog carefully, this prize that God had slipped into our garage.

I stood beside her bed, not wanting to wake her, but desperately wanting her to see the frog.

My husband and I stared at her a moment until she stirred. I cleared my throat, and she blinked her eyes.

"Mama?"

I moved closer. "I have something to show you," I whispered, holding the frog out for her to see.

She smiled and petted it, more sleepy than interested, and not the least bit surprised that her prayer had been answered.

But I was overwhelmed at the quick response to her simple prayer.

What a loving Father, to see how important such a small child's request was, a chance for her to see the power of an earnest prayer.

My faith took a leap that night as I set the frog free in our front yard. Sometimes my daughter teaches me more than I teach her.

PART TWO

"HELP ME NOT LIKE MY ANIMALS"

Children Leading

Lord, help me not to whine and cuss. [He meant fuss.]
—TIM, age five (Tim is grown up now—and is a
pastor.)

Help me to be nice to my brothers. Help my words and
tone.
—BETH, age seven

God, thank you for the peaceness. Help us have good
thinkings and no bad thinkings.
—NICHOLE, age four

The best thing about the future is, God comes with it.
—KYLE, age nine

The day had been a stressful one, and my patience had ebbed away, when my son Brett looked at me and said, "Dad. Chill."

In one word he told me to slow down, not take life—or myself—too seriously. Not bad advice.

I'm not sure I know how to chill. I see kids milling around, not doing anything, and they say they are chilling. Chilling is apparently the absence of activity, and that is something I find difficult. Yet if I am willing to follow my son's example, I just might learn this fine art. I have a feeling it will prove beneficial.

It's been said that children laugh three hundred times a day, and adults average five times a day. When it comes to enjoying life and living each moment to the fullest, we need to let our children lead the way.

Relaxing and savoring life are only two areas in which kids can and will lead, if we will take the time to listen. We can also let our kids lead us into a deeper prayer life. Kids pray about anything and everything. They don't hold back.

Perhaps we can follow their example, learn to chill, and take some time to talk with God.

Excuse me now. I'm going to go outside, hang out, and do nothing. Chill—and maybe commune with God.

—Wayne

Shirley's Story

Gloria Gaither and Shirley Dobson

from *Let's Make a Memory*

I see a little girl skipping home from school in the late afternoon sun. Her dress is a hand-me-down, intended for someone two sizes larger. Her shoes are unpolished and her socks no longer have elastic around the top. She reaches her destination and walks across a barren yard toward a small house. It is badly in need of paint and repair, but the mother who lives there can barely afford to feed and clothe her son and daughter.

How tenderly I feel for this little child of poverty. It is almost as though she were my own daughter, and I ache to hold her in my arms...to buy her a pretty new dress...to give her a shiny new bicycle. But that is impossible—for we are separated by four decades of time. I can neither talk to her nor meet her needs. For that little girl, you see, is the memory of my own childhood. I walked in her shoes. I lived in that small un-painted house. And I can still feel the indescribable yearning of a child who knew that something vital was missing from her life.

I was the daughter of a confirmed alcoholic. Only those who have lived through this nightmare will understand the full implication of this experience. I could never ask a friend to spend the night for fear my father would return in a drunken stupor and embarrass me. Night after night, he would stumble home in the early morning hours, belligerent and foul-mouthed. We would be awakened by his shouting and threats and would often hide to avoid his wrath. The rooms of our home had been patched with brown butcher paper and painted over to conceal where he had shoved his fists through the walls in fits of anger.

Like other children of an alcoholic parent, I learned to hide my disgrace. I remember being driven home from a birthday party on one occasion and asking to be left at a clean house with a well-manicured yard. I waved good-bye and marched up the driveway as if it were my own, but when the car rounded the corner, I turned and walked several blocks to my house.

It was only through the wisdom and devotion of my mother that I survived the emotional pressures of those years. She is a strong woman, and she marshaled all of her resources to hold our little family together. Since Dad spent his entire paycheck at the bar each Friday night, Mother went to work to support the family. She found a job at a fish cannery which required her to work unpredictable hours. Many times she would be called at three or four in the morning after having been kept awake all night by her harassing, drunken husband. I marveled at her ability to hold a job and to do the marketing, cooking, housekeeping, and laundry under those stressful circumstances.

Most importantly, Mom convinced my brother and me that she loved us. And because of that love, she constantly sought ways to get us through those difficult years. She had the wisdom to know that she needed help in raising two rambunctious kids, and she turned for assistance to a local evangelical church. Mom would not go with us (Sunday was her "catch up" day), but she insisted that we get involved. She would pull back the blankets every Sunday morning and order us to get ready for church. We complained and moaned, but to no avail. Mom was not a practicing Christian, but she knew that churches offered more than one kind of "salvation," and her children needed all the help they could get.

It was in that little neighborhood church that I was introduced to

Jesus Christ, and invited Him into my heart and life. He became my special friend, and I've never been the same since that moment. My pastor taught me that God cared about my personal concerns, so I began to pray for my home. My father continued to drink and associate with other women, so our situation grew steadily worse. Finally, in desperation, I went into my bedroom and cried out to God: *If Dad isn't going to change, then please get us out of this house and give us the kind of father that will love and provide for us.*

The Lord heard that prayer. After much suffering and agony involving Dad's continued drunkenness and an illicit relationship with a neighbor, my parents were divorced. I was in the sixth grade. We moved to a little shanty we called "our chicken coop," but for the first time, we could lie down in peace and enjoy an uninterrupted night's sleep.

My mother remarried a year later to a man who had been a confirmed bachelor. Joe was not a Christian at the time, but he was a man with high moral standards. We fell for his sunny disposition and big smile. He became a faithful husband and a good provider. Soon we moved to our first "real house," with bedrooms of our own and a front lawn with genuine grass and flowers. Later, both my mother and stepfather became beautiful Christians and remain committed to the faith today.

But there was another prayer that I sent toward heaven during those darkest days. As a ten-year-old girl, I began talking to God about the man I would eventually marry. I asked Him to send me a Christian husband when the time was right and not to let me fall into the private hell that my mother had experienced. Without realizing it, of course, I was praying at that moment for an eleven-year-old boy who was a thousand miles away, growing up in a loving, stable home like the one in my dreams.

My high school years proved to be relatively tranquil and I began to think about college. I enrolled in a Christian school with the financial help of my stepfather, and graduated four years later. Toward the end of my sophomore year, I began dating a tall, blond Texan named Jim Dobson. It didn't take me long to decide that he was the man I had been praying for since I was ten years old. I'll never forget the evening Jim and I were sitting in his car near the girls' dormitory, discussing our future together. He had asked me to marry him and I accepted. He turned to me and said, "I can't explain why you had to experience so much pain in your early childhood, but there is something I want you to know. I hereby pledge myself to the task of making up for those days. I am going to do the best I can to make you happy."

Jim and I soon will celebrate our thirty-fourth anniversary, and he has kept that youthful commitment. He has constructed my self-esteem as though he were a brick mason building a fortress. He has convinced me that I am a worthy person...that his love for me is unconditional, and that God has a place for me in His grand scheme for the universe. Our love for one another has never wavered throughout these three decades of daily togetherness, which is a miracle in itself. There is no doubt that God answered the second tearful prayer of a little girl named Shirley.

He also blessed us with two healthy, vibrant children and a lovely home. There are times when I stand and consider His gifts and find it difficult to realize that I am the recipient of them. Of course, to be honest, there have been difficult moments in our adult lives. We've experienced our share of reverses and sad times and illnesses. During one three-year period, for example, we lost eight members of our small family in death. But even during these times of tragedy, the presence of God has been evident to each of us. We will, after all, be united on the other side.

As I look back on the painful experience of my childhood, I am overwhelmed with gratitude to God for answering my early prayers. He heard the desperate cries of a ten-year-old girl who could offer Him nothing in return. I had no status, no special abilities, no money to contribute. My father was not a physician or a lawyer or a member of the city council. I was totally without dignity or social influence. Yet the Creator of the universe entered my little room and communed with me about the difficulties I was experiencing. It was awesome to realize that He loved me just as I was, and my pain became His pain. What a magnificent God we serve!

Is there any wonder why I believe literally in the Scripture that promises, "Trust in the Lord with all thine heart and lean not unto thine own understanding. In all thy ways acknowledge Him, and He shall direct thy paths" (Prov. 3:5–6 KJV)?

Faith in God's Living Word

Sally Clarkson

from *The Ministry of Motherhood*

T umbling out of the van on Sunday evening after two days of driving was a welcome relief to all of us, especially to the three who are six feet tall or over. (Riding together in a minivan these days has a different meaning for our family than when all my children were little.) But now that we were home, there was planning to be done. That evening found Clay and me poring over our calendars, trying to get a handle on all we needed to accomplish in the following four weeks.

We had just returned from a wonderful—and badly needed—family vacation in Florida. We had enjoyed a day together at an amusement park and spent some hours on the beach. Best of all, we had been invited to watch the launch of a space shuttle. The captain of the mission was Rick Husband, and his wife, Evelyn, is a friend of mine. So we had even been privileged to attend a prayer reception for Rick the night before.

What an inspiring time of worship and testimony that had been, with videotapes of Rick's life, magnificent music by Steve Green, and incredible pictures of outer space. Clay and I were asked to lead the corporate prayers for Rick, Evelyn, and their children, Matthew and Laura. And as we cried out in our hearts for God to give us the right words, Psalm 139 immediately came to mind.

"Lord," I prayed, "you have promised to be with us wherever we go, whether we ascend to heaven and take the wings of the dawn or dwell in the remotest part of the sea. Please help Evelyn and Matthew and Laura to remember while their husband and daddy is in outer space that you are with him. Help them to know that all of Rick's days are written in your Book. Thank you that you will be with him and protect him and be sovereign over his life because you have planned it."

As Clay began to pray, he, too, thought of a scripture: "Lord, help Matthew and Laura know that you desire to take them into your arms and bless them as you did the little children who came to you. Bless them, Lord, while their father is away, to feel the comfort of your arms" (see Matthew 19:14).

The morning of the launch had been perfect. As the space shuttle lifted off gracefully into an endless blue sky, a spontaneous round of applause had burst forth from all of us who were watching from the bleachers outside the space center. The moment had been filled with a sense of victory—a ship well launched. But now, just a few days later, we seemed to have thudded back to earth again.

I was already feeling stressed over suitcases to unpack, laundry to wash, e-mails to read, phone calls to answer, and a house waiting to be tamed the next morning. I had a feeling the next day—Monday—would be even worse. And it was.

"You know you have less than two weeks to prepare your new talks for the Michigan conference," Clay reminded me as he went out the door to his office. "And do you have time today to help me order books to sell at the book table? Also, I need someone to take my shirts to the cleaners..."

My husband's voice hadn't even faded before the litany of child voices began:

"Mom, we don't have any food in the house! What can we eat?"

"Mom, I can't find my NASA T-shirt, and I was going to wear it today! Can you help me find it?"

"Mom, I think the toilet's stopped up again. I can't get it to flush!"

"Mom, I need the car this morning! Can you stay here without a car for a while?"

The clenching of my stomach reminded me that we all needed to get our hearts in order before we tackled the tasks ahead. So I called the family together for a devotional time. And since Clay was already gone, I asked Joel if he would lead it. Though my older son was new at leading devotions, his sincere and strong heart lent strength to what he said:

"I have been reading a short passage this morning," he began when we had gathered in the living room. "It seems to apply to our lives just now. Philippians 4, verses 6 and 7." He held up his Bible and began to read: "Be anxious for nothing, but in everything by prayer and supplication with thanksgiving let your requests be made known to God. And the peace of God, which surpasses all comprehension, will guard your hearts and your minds in Christ Jesus.

"I think Paul knew we would be anxious about different areas in our lives," said Joel. (Boy, did he have that one right!) "But he tells us to take every single need that we have to God and leave it in his hands. Only then can we have the peace of Christ—when we have placed everything in his hands. He also tells us that this peace will guard our hearts and our minds. If you are letting God be God, then you will have a guard on your thoughts and feelings that will keep you from being anxious."

That was it—short and sweet. Joel led us in a prayer for our day.

"Lord, we give into your hands all the things that tempt us to be anxious. The busyness of the next few weeks. Mom and Sarah's conference in Michigan. The financial and administrative problems at the office. Our desire for friends. Lord, you know our needs. Thank you that in you we can have peace in each situation. Guard our hearts and minds through your Spirit as we trust in you. In Jesus' name, amen."

What a wonderful moment! My heart melted as my son ministered to me with heartfelt truth from God's Word that really helped me with my present needs. I had read that verse so many times before, but today it seemed to freshly apply. Off we all went to the duties of the day, sensing now that we weren't alone in the task.

Smokin' Joe

Barb Eimer

O ne of my favorite Bible stories is where Jesus blesses the little children and tells the disciples, "The kingdom of God belongs to such as these" (Mark 10:14).

He goes on to say that whoever does not receive the kingdom of God like a little child will never enter it. I've always thought this verse meant that we are to have childlike faith, and as a mom, it's easy for me to see why Jesus spoke this way. Even before my children could speak, they trusted. As they were learning to walk, they reached out and knew I would be there when they started to fall. When they were two or three, their levels of trust had expanded to such a degree that if I had told them the moon was made of cheese, they'd matter-of-factly have asked whether it was American or cheddar.

"If Mommy said it, it must be true" was their attitude, no matter how difficult an idea was for them to conceptualize. My children knew that I had their best interests at heart, so they took me at my word. I saw this time and time again, even when explaining complicated spiritual principles like the Trinity.

But the best example of childlike faith I ever saw was in my daughter, Marta. Every day on our drive to kindergarten, we passed a large billboard for Camel cigarettes, with famous Joe Camel puffing away. Marta noticed it and asked, "If smoking is bad for you, why do people put up that big sign trying to get you to do it?"

Why indeed? Of course, I did the typical mother thing and went into a lengthy diatribe about the sinful nature of man, beginning with the Fall and ending only because we arrived at school ten minutes later. Marta listened patiently to my rambling and then made this simple suggestion: "Well, Mommy, why don't we just pray that the sign falls over?"

I took a deep breath, and rather than trying to explain that we could not single-handedly right all the wrongs in the world, I just said, "Okay, Marta, let's do that."

Thus began Operation Kill the Billboard. Every time we passed the sign on the way to school, we prayed this simple prayer: "Lord, we know that this billboard advertises something that hurts our bodies and isn't good for us. Because it isn't pleasing to You, would You just take it down?"

I must confess, each time we prayed, I felt in my cold, adult-sized heart, *Fat chance this prayer has of working.*

I believe in prayer. I've seen people healed, and I know the power of God at work in my own life, but I couldn't bring myself to believe that God would do anything about the sign.

One day, after we began to pray, we noticed that Joe was starting to have problems. As we passed him, Marta said, "Mom, look! Isn't Joe tearing a little in the corner?"

Sure enough, a small strip was beginning to peel away. Each day after that, we noticed progress with more of the sign coming off in giant strips, as if a large hand was peeling wallpaper off an old wall. Naturally, we were getting excited about what God was doing.

About two weeks after our first prayer, God finished the job. Joe had vanished, and the sign was blank, except for a phone number and words at the bottom that said, "If you want to place your ad here, please call."

Marta was happy but not particularly surprised. God had done what she had asked Him to do. I have to admit, I was surprised. It was a humbling reminder that God cares about every detail of our lives and answers even the simplest of prayers.

Then it hit me why God wants us to believe like children. They see a wrong, know God can fix it, and trust that He will. They don't let the adult considerations that hinder or embarrass us stop them. Since then, whenever I'm tempted to doubt, I remember Marta's prayer. God longs to move mountains (and billboards!) if only I ask with childlike faith.

A Little Boy's Prayer

Janet Sketchley

Tired and discouraged, I steered the car through a cold, windy winter's night. I'd already let one of my sons down; it wouldn't do to be late for his brother.

My husband was away on business, leaving me alone with two active preschoolers. This was five-year-old Adam's night to attend Pioneer Clubs at a nearby church. Two-year-old Andrew and I had dropped him off and gone shopping to fill the hour until it was time to collect him.

It wasn't until I was buckling Andrew back into his car seat that I realized his doily was missing. No traditional panda for this boy; he snuggled a lacy, crocheted table centerpiece of multicolored cotton thread. Something about the texture—and the taste—soothed him.

Now his treasure was gone. Much love and frequent washing had frayed its edges. Our friends knew its value, but to a stranger it would be only a colorful rag.

Andrew took it everywhere, a combination soother and security blanket. He was fine now, but what would happen when he needed comfort? How would I get him to sleep tonight?

I snatched him out of the car and dashed through both stores, retracing our earlier carefree wanderings. A kind employee in the second store noticed my frantic search. My voice was shaky with unshed tears as I described the lost doily and explained its importance. Andrew smiled at her engagingly, his blue eyes shining.

We looked on and under shelves without success. Without much hope, I left my name and phone number with the clerk. How could I have lost track of Andrew's security doily? *What kind of a mother was I?*

Ten minutes later I helped Adam into the car, apologizing for being late. His big brown eyes never left my face as I told him about the lost doily. I finished, choking back a sob.

He placed a mittened hand on my arm and announced that we had to pray—right away. In the almost empty parking lot, we bowed our heads and asked God to help find Andrew's special doily.

Adam's "amen" was clear and confident. To him the problem was solved. I stared out at the darkness and wondered how to prepare my son to learn that sometimes God says no.

The boys were too tired to go back to the stores. At home we were partway through our bedtime routine when a friend dropped in for a visit. I gave him a cup of tea, then excused myself to finish getting my sons to bed.

I dug out Andrew's spare doily and settled both children for the night, praying one doily would be enough. At least he hadn't insisted on one for each hand tonight, but I knew if it fell behind his crib or got lost in his blankets he'd wake up screaming.

With a much-needed cup of tea in hand, I rejoined my friend in the living room just as the phone rang. The store clerk had found Andrew's ragtag doily. In my panic I had given her the wrong number, but she cared enough to look me up in the directory.

Leaving my bemused bachelor friend guarding my two still-alert boys in their beds, I sped to the store to claim my prize. I was so thankful—to God and to the sympathetic woman at the store. More than that, I was humbled by a little boy's faith that far outshone my own.

Sometimes God *does* say no, but Adam taught me that sometimes

God says *yes*. What gave my son's prayer the power mine lacked? I looked at the circumstances and tried to be realistic. Adam looked at God and expected help. God hears the prayers of frazzled mothers, but this time I think He delighted to honor the simple confidence of a child.

Listening Prayers

Jennifer A. Schuchmann

For a brief time our children think what we think. They like what we like. They do what we say. Then comes a moment somewhere between the ages of two and four when they do or say something that is uniquely theirs. The first time my son, Jordan, voiced his own opinion, I joked to my husband, "Who said he could have a mind of his own?" Yet even as I teased, I also mourned the declining influence I would have on his life.

Jordan's independence brought with it new insights beyond the things I had taught him. Nowhere was this more evident than in his prayers. He noticed things I didn't, such as when his music teacher was depressed and needed encouragement or when his dad had a frustrating day at work or when friends were anxious about upcoming travel plans. He would pray aloud about those people and their concerns, and I would feel ashamed that I hadn't been listening to the needs of those around me.

This was particularly evident the day he heard God calling him.

Jordan was mesmerized by the cartoon on the television in my bedroom. But his concentration broke when I walked by.

"Did you call me?" he asked.

"No, I just came upstairs to collect the laundry."

"Did you call my name when I was in the shower?"

I looked at his dripping face and smelled the shampoo that obviously hadn't been rinsed from his hair. *Why didn't he ever towel off?* He had his pajamas on, but he was so wet, he had soaked through his pj's.

"No, I didn't say anything."

"Is Dad home?"

"No, he's still working," I answered as I sorted whites from darks.

"Oh. Then it must have been God."

I put the laundry down and sat next to him on the floor. "What must have been God, honey?"

"When I was in the shower somebody said 'Jordan, Jordan,' and it sounded like God."

"Could it have been the TV?"

"Nope, it was God."

He seemed so sure that I asked, "What does He sound like?"

"He has a deep voice."

"Could it have been the thunder? There's a storm outside."

"Nope, it was God," he said confidently. "Besides I didn't turn the TV on until I got out of the shower, and God doesn't sound like thunder."

My son was convinced that he had just heard God's voice. I picked up a sweat sock to toss into the laundry basket, but instead I began to twist it. *Was my child hearing God?*

"Did He say anything else?"

"Nope, just 'Jordan, Jordan.'" With that he ended the conversation and returned to his cartoons.

I put the stretched-out sock into the basket and tried to convince myself that it was thunder, the television, or even some sort of storm-related power surge. I thought about other possibilities but realized there wasn't a good explanation.

Could God have spoken to Jordan? If so, what did it mean?

The more I tried to talk myself out of this possibility, the more I began to feel guilty for trying to spread my doubts. If God had spoken to Jordan, I should celebrate his faith rather than persuade him differently.

Over the next few days I quietly watched Jordan. For the first time I began to notice the things he noticed—the teachers who were having a difficult day, the neighborhood boy who was acting out because of an impending move, and the subtle shifts in my husband's mood in the evening. I listened as Jordan, in his childlike way, processed those observations in his prayers. "God, please help Ms. P know that she's a good teacher, help Hunter to stay in his house, and help my dad at work tomorrow 'cause it's tax season."

As I tucked him under his jungle-themed comforter and kissed him on the forehead, I realized the difference between Jordan's prayers and mine. His petitions came from listening to those around him. He simply paid attention. In his unassuming way, Jordan heard the needs of others. He also heard when God called his name.

As I turned out his light and said, "Love you, good night," I realized that prayer is two-way communication. To be heard, you also have to listen.

By listening, perhaps even *I* could hear God's call.

OF TEDDY BEARS AND MISSIONARIES

Sharon Hinck

W here's Joel?" I asked as I dried the last dish from our Sunday lunch. My husband grabbed the plate to tuck into the cupboard and shrugged. His radar wasn't tuned to go on high alert as quickly as mine. I knew that too many minutes of silence from our seven-year-old usually meant that trouble was brewing.

Katie, our kindergartner, practiced somersaults on the living-room rug and sang "Fishers of Men" to herself. The theme in Sunday school that morning had been missions, and she was still in the spirit of things.

"Katie, where's Joel?"

She peered up at me from a headstand. Freeing one pudgy hand, she waved toward the stairs. "His room." Then she toppled over with a giggle.

I paused in the stairwell and listened. Suspicious silence blanketed the attic bedrooms. No clash of LEGOs falling. No zooming Hot Wheels. What was he up to?

I tiptoed up the stairs and saw my son hunched on the edge of his bed, head bowed. "Honey, are you okay?"

Knuckles rubbed his cheek before he lifted his eyes. "Yeah. I was just thinking."

I stepped over his model castle and pushed aside a few padded dinosaurs on his quilt to clear a spot next to him. My arm wrapped around him. "What are you thinking about?"

"That guy in church."

A visiting missionary had delivered the sermon that morning. He gave an impassioned appeal to be open to God's leading in our lives—particularly if He directs us toward evangelism.

Joel turned his earnest eyes my way. "What if God asks me to be a missionary?" Worry radiated from his young face.

"Then He'd give you the strength to do it." I used my sage and eternally wise mom voice.

Joel shook his head and grabbed a teddy bear, one furry favorite from his treasured zoo of toys. "But Mom, the man said we had to be willing to give things up to serve God. I prob'ly couldn't take my stuffed animals." He sniffed and squeezed the bear. "So I've been praying. I know God should be more important to me than my animals." Tears pooled in his blue eyes.

I struggled to find a theological answer to the question of stuffed animals and sacrifice in the life of a Christian. "Sweetie, God understands how much you love your toys. If He calls you to a mission field one day, He'll either give you peace in your heart about leaving them or help you find a way to bring them." I glanced at the large pile of fuzzy creatures on his bed and decided that would be a pretty impressive miracle.

Joel blinked up at me. "I asked God to help me not like my animals so much. But I still do."

I squeezed his shoulder. "That's because He's not calling you to a foreign mission today. When I surrendered my life to God, I was afraid I'd have to give up everything I cared about. Instead, He keeps giving me more new things to love. I've had to say good-bye to some things, but He's helped me. You don't need to worry. He'll help you when the time comes."

Joel heaved a big sigh, then sprang from the bed. "Cool. Can I bike around the block?"

"Yes, but wear your helmet."

He was already charging down the stairs and yelling to Katie to play outside with him.

I propped up a few droopy rabbits, a rotund bear with a bow tie, and one fluorescent turtle—the only witnesses to a little boy's conversations with God. My heart filled as I thought of how quickly he was growing up and exploring his own walk with Jesus.

Joel wasn't the only one pondering the sacrifices of love. My life was full of teddy bears too—possessions, habits, and roles I found hard to surrender to God. Joel's example reminded me to trust God enough to relinquish the things I clutched to my heart. There among the collection of furry toys, I bowed my head for my own time of prayer.

PART THREE

"When I Grow Up"

Children Playing

Lord, please give me a vision. I want to see You.

—ANNEMARIE, age six

I'm glad You made puppies and kittens, baby horses, and
bunnies, Lord. They remind me that You really love small
things like me.

—SARAH, age eight

God, thank You for letting me spend the night and watch
a scary movie with Papa. And thank You God for the
candy Papa gave me. Amen.

—ALEC, age four

If you want to be something wonderful, be yourself.

—ALYSSA, age twelve

T he line between playing and praying is not always clear—at least not with kids.

I recall sitting in a church service with my parents when I was very young, listening to the minister invite people to come to the front for prayer. People went forward (some were crying as they did), knelt, and prayed. When they finished they returned to their seats, and I noticed a distinct change in them. They were happy and at peace. I looked to my dad for an explanation, but he only motioned me to be silent.

Finally a day came when I looked to my dad, and he bent down to speak. "Would you like to go forward?" he asked. I nodded my affirmation. Like those who had gone before, I knelt, prayed, and cried. Before long I felt better too, and I sensed the time had come to return to my seat. My dad smiled. My little world and I were at peace. I didn't want to ever leave that place or lose that feeling.

A week later the minister again invited people to come forward. I asked my dad if I could go again. He approved, and once again I found the peace I had felt the week before. This pattern continued for several weeks, until one Sunday my dad explained to me that it wasn't necessary to go forward every time.

My dad probably sensed my disappointment, but his guidance had been so tender that I didn't want him to see my sadness. I smiled and hugged his leg.

Reflecting on that incident, I believe I saw the prayer time to be a form of play. It was fun. It made me feel good—just like play. And perhaps most prayer and worship begin for children as an extension of play.

Maybe we should go back to that time to discover the pure joy of being in the presence of the heavenly Father. Our cares will be lighter if we relearn how to play in the presence of God, to let our prayers be an extension of the joy that comes from being with the One who knows us, loves us, and accepts us unconditionally.

I don't want my prayer time to feel like work. I want it to be fun. When I am through, I want to feel the joy that comes from being in His presence. Just like when I was a kid, I never want to leave that place or lose that feeling. I want to be a child of prayer once more.

—Wayne

DIVINE INTERRUPTIONS

Patty Stump

A s I cracked open our front door, my eyes were met by the sparkling blue eyes of the four-year-old boy from next door. "Can I come in and play?" he asked.

Before I could respond, our three-year-old daughter, Elisabeth, swung the door open and enthusiastically escorted her friend across the freshly mopped kitchen floor to the toy box in the corner of the neatly organized family room. Hmm, so much for my plans.

In a less-than-inviting tone, I said to our guest, "Come on in. But if you're going to play over here, you two cannot get out any toys, mess up the family room, turn on the TV, or clutter the kitchen." Elisabeth undoubtedly picked up on my demeanor and wisely whisked our little visitor from the family room to the more inviting surroundings of our covered patio. At least now I could remop the kitchen in peace.

As the children headed out the sliding-glass door, I attempted to pick back up where I'd left off. Now, where was I? The family room was organized, the kitchen was almost spotless, and the toy box was finally free from clutter. I certainly hoped I wouldn't be interrupted again with requests for Kool-Aid, snacks, or lunch. I didn't want to add sticky fingers, juice stains, or muddy footprints to my ever-growing list of tasks to tend to.

Glancing out the patio door, I noticed the children sitting Indian style, facing each other. It certainly didn't look as if our neighbor was in a hurry to go home. I couldn't help but focus on the fact that if he stayed too long, things would get messed up all over again, and my entire morning would have been wasted.

Frustration welled up within me as I mulled over the anticipated impact our uninvited guest would have upon my plans. I found myself wondering why he didn't go and mess up his own house. Finally, enough was enough. I set aside my mop and marched toward the patio with the intent of ushering the little fellow in the direction of his house. As I headed for the door, I began to announce my plans to my daughter.

"Elisabeth. Elisabeth. It's time for—"

Before I could finish my sentence, Elisabeth gently responded, "Mom, just a minute. I was telling him about Jesus living in my heart. He wants to ask Jesus into his heart too, Mommy. Do you want to pray with us?"

I was stunned. "I, uhh, I'll be right back."

As I left the patio, I overheard Elisabeth asking her friend to bow his head and repeat after her: "Dear Jesus, I want You to come into my heart. Please forgive me for…"

So much for my priorities and pursuits. I'd been so consumed with my agenda that I'd been unable to see God's hand in the midst of the interruptions. Elisabeth jolted my thoughts as she stuck her head around the corner of the door and asked, "Mom, can we play together a little longer?"

Suddenly my list of "to-dos" didn't seem quite as urgent. I realized that God had placed before me a special moment I could choose to embrace or carelessly brush aside. After taking a deep breath, I pulled out some paper plates and peanut butter, poured two tall glasses of Kool-Aid, and set up the patio table with a simple lunch for the playmates. As they finished their meal, I unexpectedly found myself wanting Elisabeth's friend to stay a little bit longer. Without a moment's hesitation I asked, "Would anyone like to make some sugar cookies?"

◄◦►◄◦►

Elisabeth's priorities and heartfelt prayer for her little friend transformed our otherwise ordinary moments into an afternoon marked by a divine encounter. The Lord used the faith and availability of our small daughter to draw a needy neighbor to Himself.

As the afternoon came to a close, I, too, recognized my need to seek the Lord in prayer. I asked Him to help me be more discerning regarding where I invest my time and energies and to more readily recognize the difference between what's truly important and the seemingly urgent. I also asked Him to help me embrace the interruptions of life as opportunities for Him to work in and through my circumstances in such a way that others will catch a glimpse of the countenance of Christ right in their midst.

"When I Grow Up"

Robert Benson

from *Between the Dreaming and the Coming True*

I have a private theory that mothers have been genetically blessed when it comes to singing camp songs. So when I am alone in the car with my two young children, we very often play a game called When I Grow Up I Am Gonna Be _____. It is exactly the kind of Winnie-the-Pooh sort of game that a camp-song-challenged father would make up to pass the time when a six-year-old daughter and a four-year-old son are getting restless.

The rules of the game are simple. On the first round, you go from player to player, each one declaring what they want to be when they grow up. On the next round, each one describes some aspect of what it will be like to be that—where you might live, what you might wear, what kind of shoes it takes, and so forth. The object is to keep remembering what you have been saying. When you leave out any one of the things on your list, you are out of the game.

"When I grow up, I'm gonna be a cowboy," I said, leading off one day. I like to start, hoping that one day what will come out of my mouth is what I might actually be when I grow up.

My daughter quickly said, "When I grow up, I'm gonna be a cheerleader."

From the backseat, my son sang out, "When I grow up, I'm gonna be a fireman." He loves this game. He has a great affinity for the uniforms that go with various occupations. If he is going to be a pirate, he dresses the part before he goes out to play. When he changes games, he changes clothes. The makers of Tide consider him to be at the very center of their marketing strategy.

Round and round we went. "When I grow up, I am gonna be a cowboy and have a white horse and I will have a black hat and I am gonna live on a big ranch in Montana," I said.

"When I grow up, I'm gonna be a cheerleader and wear white cheerleading shoes and cheer for Vanderbilt and do flips whenever we score a basket," said my daughter.

My son was in the middle of his fireman with a red hat and polka-dotted dog and ladder truck round. But four rounds is about the maximum for him, and from the backseat there was a tentative beginning. "When I grow up, I'm gonna be...uh, uh..." and then a long and painful pause.

During the pause my daughter got excited because she knew that one of her competitors was about to go down in defeat. My son began to get a look of resignation on his face as he foresaw his impending elimination from the contest. And I started into the hint routine I often performed in the rearview mirror, hoping my son would see me mouthing the word *fireman*. But he was not looking at me; his eyes were closed in concentration as a few minutes went by slowly.

Suddenly his face brightened, and with a big grin, the grin of the suddenly all-knowing, Geoffrey announced, "When I grow up I am going to be *Geoffrey!*" We declared him world champion for life right on the spot.

―◦►―◦►―

Editor's Note: Although Robert Benson's story about his son, Geoffrey, does not include a prayer, I wanted to include it in this collection because of the insight Geoffrey brings—and also to offer a prayer on his behalf. In our lives we often aspire to be many things and to accomplish many tasks. When I grow up, I hope to write books, and have a book make the best-seller list, and have a movie made from one of my books.

My prayer is that, like Geoffrey, I won't forget to be Wayne—the Wayne God created me to be. So the prayer I offer on Geoffrey's behalf is that God would help us be true to who we are, no matter what tasks we set out to accomplish.

"Sewing" Seeds of Faith

Joy Brown

Afternoon naptime had arrived. I gently laid our baby daughter, Molly, in her crib for what I knew would be a few hours of sleep. I was trying to complete a sewing project, and I felt sure I could accomplish a lot during that time of peace and quiet.

I turned to tuck our older daughter, Meri Beth, in bed. However, I could tell by her wide-eyed "What are we going to do now, Mommy?" expression that a nap was not an option for her.

Compromising, I said, "Let's go upstairs. You can get some toys from the playroom and bring them beside the sewing machine. Then you can play while I sew."

As I held her hand and climbed the stairs, I could sense her excitement. She had avoided the dreaded nap.

We went into the big closet that had been converted into a playroom, and Meri Beth carefully selected toys to bring beside my sewing machine. She sat on the floor playing as I resumed work on my project. A few minutes later she jumped up and said, "I'll get my toy sewing machine, and I'll sew with you."

I assured her that was a good idea, so I gave her some scraps of cloth to "sew." She ran into the playroom, and I could hear toys being moved as she shuffled through her treasures looking for the toy sewing machine. After a while she came out of the room and said despondently, "I can't find it. Will you come and help me?"

We went into the playroom and looked together in every conceivable place. We took toys out of the toy chest. We looked under things. We moved everything in the entire room, and the toy sewing machine was not to be found. I went downstairs and looked quietly in the room where Molly was napping, but it wasn't there. Since we had recently moved to that home, I surmised it had been misplaced in the move.

"I'm sorry. I'm afraid your sewing machine might have gotten lost. You can play with something else while I sew."

Meri Beth sat back down beside me and began playing with the toys she had chosen originally. Suddenly she looked up and said, "I know. I'll just ask Jesus." Then with complete confidence she prayed, "Jesus, please show me where my sewing machine is."

She scurried back into the playroom. I sat at the sewing machine, cupped my face in my hands and began praying. I knew the toy sewing machine was not there.

Heavenly Father, please give me the words I need to explain that not all of our prayers are answered in the way we think they should be. She's young, and this could be a crucial point in her faith and her understanding of You. Help me know what to say and how to say it when she cannot find her sewing machine.

As I sat there praying I was aware of her presence beside me. I turned to look, and there she sat with the toy sewing machine and her scrap of cloth already in place so she could join me in sewing.

"Where did you find your sewing machine?"

Puzzled by my bewilderment, she said, "I walked back in the room, and it was right there on the floor in front of me."

When I left the room, the floor was clear. When she reentered the room, her sewing machine was waiting for her.

My prayer had been for guidance to explain faith. Her prayer had simply been one of faith.

I can't explain how the sewing machine appeared. I only know that it did. God used a trusting child and a toy to plant a seed of faith in the heart of this mother. I understood more clearly that "of such is the kingdom of heaven."

GOD *Is* WITH US

Peggy Morris

T hat's not fair! You always get to sit there," griped Christopher to his older brother, Wes.

"No, I don't!" Wes said. "You're being a big baby, and you always want *your* way."

"I'm not a baby!" Christopher said. "You're just a bully!"

Grumpy and Grouchy. These are the names I'd have to assign my *typically* well-mannered little boys when they gathered around the dinner table one evening.

To convince them to quit arguing, I first tried my calm-but-forceful, "Now, boys, that's enough" approach, but almost immediately I knew, *This is not going to work.* I stood up, marched over to a nearby chair, pulled it up to the table, and asked, "Jesus, will You come have a seat in this chair and join us for dinner?"

Having never seen me do anything like this before, the boys responded with complete silence. Apparently the simple reminder of Jesus's presence among us had invoked a sense of reverence in their hearts. That became evident as Wes began saying grace over the food.

"Dear Jesus, I'm sorry for acting ugly, and thanks for the food. Amen."

After prayer, the boys' grumpy attitudes immediately changed for the better. And because of it, we all enjoyed a delightfully delicious family meal together.

Weeks later we invited a family from our church over for dinner. After they arrived we gathered chairs to seat everyone around the table. This included the chair that Jesus sat in. With everyone seated, my husband began returning thanks for the food, and as he did, I could feel our youngest son Christopher tapping me gently on the leg. Assuming he wanted to be excused to use the rest room, I bent down so he could whisper. With one little hand cupped over my ear and the other pointing to *the chair,* he whispered, "Mom, she's sitting in Jesus's lap!"

Through their acceptance of the chair as Jesus's chair, the boys learned a valuable lesson many of us would do well to remember. The Lord is present at all times and longs to be included in every meal and moment of life.

WEE-ONES WORSHIP

Kelly Hayes

P raise the Lord, Praise the Lord, let the *people* rejoice; Praise the Lord, Praise the Lord, let the *eagles* rejoice," I heard my five-year-old daughter sing as she and her three-year-old brother played church in the next room. Working to fix lunch, I crept about the kitchen quietly. Too many clanks of a spoon or knife and I'd reveal my secret listening post— a guaranteed way to bring my children's play to an end, a guaranteed way to miss other great one-liners from my coed comic team.

Apparently I finished making peanut-butter-and-jelly sandwiches just in time, because the prayer following "To God Be the Glory" came from what sounded like a hungry child. My daughter prayed, "Dear Lord, bless us! We must get our food and drinks!"

Thinking that was my cue to serve lunch, I was surprised to peek in and discover that my kids had their own version of lunch in mind. My daughter presided behind their makeshift communion table—a heavy-duty, plastic, chunky-style kids' table—preparing saltine crackers and grape juice. She served her brother, who sat right up and ate. Then they switched places so he could have a turn serving Communion.

Immediately following this second Communion service, my daughter hopped up again and lost no time announcing the sermon. She began her lesson with "We don't know when Jesus was born, and we don't know where He was born. Actually, we *do* know where He was born. And then His family had to move to Nazareth. And they were very happy there. But then Jesus had to die. But He comes back again every year at Christmas. Ho ho ho!"

I bolted back to the kitchen, barely containing my laughter, and silently thanked God for the gift of children and their humor. Sometimes I get so wrapped up in appearances and trying to do things perfectly that I miss the meaning and joy of life. Sometimes when things don't go the way *I* think they should, focusing on the imperfection blinds me to the freedom. God wants us to enjoy our worship of Him like children playing church. He created us for worship and wants us to glorify and enjoy Him forever.

My worship is far from perfect. Sometimes I mess up on the words to a song and mix up my Bible facts. That's when I thank God for His grace, His perfect sense of humor, and the unexpected blessing of old shag carpeting. Without it, I *never* would have let my kids take grape juice in the living room. And chances are excellent that I would have missed out on witnessing my children's genuine, heartfelt worship. Thank You, God, for giving me playful children—and old, ugly carpet.

EMMA'S PLACE

Jennifer A. Schuchmann

R oni and John's friends arrived early on Saturday morning carrying crowbars, sledgehammers, and other tools of destruction to tear down the second-floor deck before the Georgia sun took away the shade of the large pine trees in the backyard.

Though Emma was only four, she knew the activity was for her.

"Dorothy, guess what?" Emma said peering into the fish bowl where Dorothy lived. "Daddy and the men are making a special place for me outside. But you can come too."

Roni watched Emma's delicate features reflect off the fish bowl, exaggerating her large brown eyes and porcelain skin. Sometimes Roni wondered how they could protect a daughter who seemed so fragile. "Do you want to help Mommy get some drinks for the workers?"

Always ready to help, Emma said good-bye to Dorothy and followed her mother to the kitchen.

The men had already started tearing up the floor. Stripping the deck went quickly. During a brief break Emma helped serve bottled sports drinks, then she and her mother gingerly trod through the splintered boards, scrap metal, and tools that littered the back lawn to get to the screen porch where they could safely watch the men at work.

John and his friends turned to the thick boards that once held the flooring in place. Standing on the ground, the men reached overhead to the first story to pound and pry until the joist loosened. They stood back while one man took the final whack before each board broke free from the house. The rusted nails and sun-weathered trusses broke loose in predictable patterns, but as the men beat on the joist, a small board broke free and fell, narrowly missing one of the workers.

"Mommy, we need to pray for the men."

Roni glanced down at her daughter and smiled. "That's right, baby."

Emma and Roni often prayed together. On Sundays they would pray for other churches on the way to their own. When they heard sirens, they prayed for those who were hurt or in trouble as well as for their families. They prayed every night at bedtime, and Emma could pray aloud with the best of the preschoolers, but this was the first time she initiated.

"With our eyes closed, okay?"

"Okay." Roni smiled as she took Emma's hand and watched her close her eyes and bow her head. Roni prayed, but with her eyes open watching the men attack the stubborn joist.

"Dear God, can You please make them to be safe and don't let men get hurt? Don't make men get hurt."

Roni squeezed her daughter's hand and said amen.

"A-men," said Emma.

―◦―◦―

Chunks of wood rained down on John's head as he and the other men kept up the barrage against the stubborn joists. Removing the decking and the first four joists had been easy. Only a few boards remained before the old deck would be kindling.

John lifted the sledgehammer over his head and brought it down on the side of the beam. Between blows he could hear his daughter, Emma, praying from the sunroom above. Though she was only four, her precise way of articulating words made her seem refined beyond her years. John pictured the fun she would have in the new playhouse that would replace the area where the deck once stood.

He reached up to slam the hammer down again. The wood creaked. It was almost time for the blow that would bring the joist down. He heard his wife's voice mix with Emma's. He smiled and listened to her simple petition. *Someday,* he thought, *Emma will learn the difference between prayers that are nice and those that are needed.* This was nice, but he didn't really need her prayer; they had only a few more beams to go, and they would be done.

He took another whack. The two-by-ten shifted. The men knew the next blow would bring it down. His partner signaled that he would make the final strike, and John turned to walk under the sunroom just as Emma finished her prayer.

"A-men," said the little voice from above.

The last whack of the hammer loosened the joist from the house. As the board slammed into John's shoulder, he was forced to the ground. The pain was immediate. John found it difficult to breathe and thought it was because the beam was still on top of him. As he struggled to get up, he realized that the board had rolled off and was lying next to him. It wasn't the weight of the beam that made breathing difficult; it was the pain from the blow.

John's friend reached out a hand and held on until John was steady.

"I'm okay," said John, though he wasn't sure he believed it. The pain was intense as he stretched his arms and turned his head, but there didn't seem to be anything broken, and he wasn't bleeding. He bent over to pick up his sledgehammer. "Let's get it done," he said to his friends.

Hours later he thanked them and said good-bye, but he could still feel the burning in his shoulder.

"Let me see it," Roni said, pulling up his shirt. "It's really bruised. You can see where the corner of the board hit you." She traced the blue and green bruise with her finger. "I can't believe it. Emma and I were praying for you and the men right when it happened, but you still got hurt. You'd think God would hear a child's prayer."

John pulled his shirt down. "Just as Emma said amen, the board fell on me. This wasn't a coincidence. God heard her prayer. Come here, let me show you something."

They walked to the backyard where the lumber lay in piles, ready for removal. John kicked the board over with his foot. "See that?" Because the joist had held the flooring in place, nails stuck out every two or three inches all the way down the ten-foot plank. "That's the side that *didn't* hit me."

"John, if those nails had gone into your shoulder—"

"Or the board had fallen on my head instead of my back? I could have been seriously hurt. Look at where it fell from," he said, pointing up. "Think about the weight of that two-by-ten and how fast it fell."

"It didn't even break the skin."

"I'm glad you decided to pray."

"It wasn't my idea. That's what I was going to tell you. It was Emma's idea. I didn't even prompt her." Roni studied the rusty nails. "Maybe God did."

"The timing was pretty incredible. I heard you and Emma say amen, and she sounded so sincere. Then, *wham!* that board hit me."

"I guess God heard her prayers after all."

As they walked toward the house, Roni asked, "Do you have any other bruises?"

"Only my ego."

Roni smiled. "I meant did you get hurt anywhere else?"

"I know what you meant, but I didn't think I needed prayer. I thought

I was safe. Now I have to ask myself how many times has God prompted me to pray and I've ignored His voice because I didn't think I needed to."

"Maybe as many times as I thought He wasn't listening to our prayers?" responded Roni. "I guess Emma knows where real protection comes from."

"We're the parents, and we're supposed to be teaching her, but today she taught both of us."

"It's kind of funny. Here we were fixing up the backyard as a place for Emma to play, and instead she made it a place to pray."

PART FOUR

"I FOUND IT"

Children Believing

Please forgive me of my bad sins. Please make my heart whiter than snow. Throw my sins into the deepest part of the ocean. Draw me close with Your love. Please make my heart sparkle with Your love, Your goodness, Your kindness, and Your mercy.

> —MOLLY, age seven

Dear God, every Christmas I ask for a pet. Thank You for finally answering my prayer.

> —WILL, age ten, who got a bunny last Christmas

You're better than a collection of a gazillion stickers. You're also better than a kitchen full of all my favorite things to eat and sometimes that's Froot Loops and Fritos.

> —SARAH, age seven

C hildren believe. Without the skepticism and doubts that adults carry wherever they go, children simply believe. Tell a child that God answers prayer, and he or she will put your words to the test, often with remarkable results.

As I was preparing this book, the kids' stories reminded me of a valuable lesson. Children are very specific when they pray. If their family is short two hundred dollars on their mortgage payment, they don't ask God to "meet their needs" or "provide for their family." Instead, they ask God to send them two hundred dollars.

I'm reminded of four-year-old Dana, the daughter of a writer-friend, who prayed, "Dear Jesus, help us not to eat slugs."

Now that's praying specifically.

My prayers, on the other hand, are often too general. I pray for my children, but not with concreteness. I pray for my friends, but again, I don't always pray for specific needs. I want to follow the example of children because I've discovered that when you pray specific prayers, God gives you specific answers.

Kids believe. I want to regain the simple childlike faith that knows God answers prayer. Ask Him, and be specific.

—Wayne

THE LOST CONTACT

Kay Arthur

from *Lord, Teach Me to Pray in 28 Days*

H ave you ever been embarrassed or even afraid to pray for things in a definite way for fear God wouldn't answer your prayer? I have. I have thought, "Father, what if You don't answer this prayer? It's going to look like prayer doesn't work!" At this point some of you may be laughing at me... I don't blame you, because I'm laughing too! I can hear you saying, "Kay, why put the blame on God if the prayer is not answered? Why not put it on yourself?"

I'll tell you why! I felt I was claiming faith in His character and His ways and if God didn't come through, it really would look like He had failed! Honestly! That is the way I felt. Let me give you an illustration. This one is from my early days as a Christian, when I was about three or four years old in the Lord. Since then I have come to trust my Father more and to relax in His ways.

Jack and I were missionaries in Mexico and had taken a group of English-speaking teens on a weekend retreat. Conditions were really primitive, but the girls had the best end of the deal. We had an army surplus tent over our heads.

That night as we sat around the campfire and I taught, God really spoke. Several missionary kids who thought they were saved came to the Lord that evening. I am wary of emotional decisions around campfires, so I did not offer an invitation. Even so, from out of the dark they came to me, separately, many in tears, telling me they had turned to God and were willing to follow Him totally. God had moved! (Time eventually proved the reality of these commitments.)

Well, you can imagine the joy in the tent that night. You know how girls are! They were at fever pitch when all of a sudden we heard a loud, agonized, "Oh, no! I've dropped my contact! My parents will kill me." Now you know missionary parents are not allowed to kill their children because it's a bad testimony! However, Gail was probably right—it might have crossed their minds. The lost contact was a brand-new one she had gotten to replace another one she had just lost! Replacing contacts is hard on missionary support funds!

At any rate, we were all down on our knees with lanterns held above our heads as we looked in green grass for a green-tinted contact! And at that moment God reminded me that I had just been teaching these teens about Him, His attributes, and His ways. "Ask Me to find it," came the thought. "Ask Me in front of the girls."

A silent debate ensued. "But, Father, what if I ask You and we don't find it? How is that going to look?" I went back to my groping, but I couldn't help thinking, "He does know where it is because He is omniscient, all-knowing. There is not a thing hidden from His sight." Still I resisted; it was too risky. We might not find it. Then how would God look? I had better not risk His reputation in front of ones so young in the faith. (Can you understand what I was going through?)

Well, God won. I prayed. As I did, I reminded Him fervently of every promise I could think of that related to our plight.

After I finished, we continued to search for a while to the intermittent tune of Gail's swan song, one short chorus, "My parents are gonna kill me! My parents are gonna kill me!"

When I was almost ready to tell God I never should have prayed aloud, Lily let out a hysterical yelp, "I found it! I found it!" Tears poured down her face. But why? These weren't gushy, sentimental, girlish tears.

I didn't have to wait long to find out. Of all the teens, none was more exemplary in behavior or zeal for missions than Lily. Any one of us would have willingly claimed her as our own. She would have made us look like ideal missionary parents! Lily claimed to have been saved at a very young age, and her behavior gave us no cause to doubt the reality of her profession. Yet here was that precious girl, tears streaming down her face, half-laughing and half-crying as she told us her story.

After the lesson around the campfire, Lily realized she really had never been saved. It was hard for her to believe, since she had led so many others to Christ. Yet she knew it was true, so there in the dark the transaction had taken place. Lily had passed from death to life, from the power of Satan to the Kingdom of God. She had received forgiveness of sins and an inheritance among those who are sanctified (Acts 26:18). She had been coming into the tent to tell us when Gail went into hysterics over her contact.

While I was on my knees looking for the contact and wrestling with God about praying aloud, Lily was praying: "O God, You have never directly answered my prayers all these years. Now that I am Yours, prove it by answering this prayer. Let me find Gail's contact."

Does God always find lost contacts when we pray? I know of some cases where He hasn't, even though those who prayed sincerely believed. Why did He find Gail's? Because I believed? No. Because it was His will—and in this instance we prayed according to His will.

Think on it. Pray about it. The will of God is a key to solving many mysteries regarding prayer. What have you been asking God for? Did you ask Him first if it was His will? If not, then why don't you spend time in prayer asking Him to show you His will?

CALLED TO DELIVER OTHERS

Heather Whitestone McCallum and Angela Hunt

from *Let God Surprise You*

A few days ago I read a moving newspaper article about a family that adopted eight children from an orphanage in Russia. With two biological children already, the adoption expanded their family to twelve—and they lived in a three-bedroom ranch house. I couldn't understand why they would take in so many children.

But as I kept reading, I realized that they did not set out to adopt eight children. Their mission of mercy—to deliver these children from distressing circumstances and give them a home—unfolded over time, as God showed them the need. Adopting children wasn't part of their plan at all until after the tragic car-accident death of their biological son, only a day shy of his tenth birthday. The idea was planted by their daughter who later commented, "Our family would never be right with just two children." In time the parents went to Russia and brought home a sibling pair, a brother and a sister.

During the first year, their newly adopted daughter cried herself to sleep every night because she missed her best friend, a girl still at the Russian orphanage. She explained that the two of them had always held hands at night until they fell asleep. Having mercy on this heartbroken child, the mother went back to Russia to find the best friend. Once there, she discovered that the girl had two brothers. She did not have the heart to separate a sibling group, so she brought all three children home.

In the meantime, their first adopted son announced that he had been praying that his new family would adopt his other three sisters, who still lived with their biological parents. The American mother tried to explain that this was impossible; they couldn't go to Russia and "take" the three girls. But that didn't keep the boy from praying.

And his prayer was answered. Can you imagine how surprised this American family was to receive news from Russia? The three sisters were suddenly available for adoption, abandoned by their mother after their father had been killed in a fire. Once again, the American mother packed her bags and boarded a jet plane. When she arrived in Russia, one of the three sisters recognized her from a photo at the children's home. "I always dreamed I would meet you," she said.

These missions of mercy may or may not have saved the children's lives, but they illustrate how God frequently works to deliver people in distress as we make ourselves available to be agents of deliverance.*

---

* Sheila Poole, "A Family Value," *The Atlanta Journal-Constitution* (29 May 2002): E1.

LOOKING FOR T. T.

Linda Knight

For five years, every day when I woke up and came down the stairs, T. T. would come running to greet me, tail wiggling with excitement, her motor purring full tilt. This day it was raining, but T. T. stood meowing at the back door insisting that I let her out. T. T. loved the outdoors. She especially enjoyed chasing butterflies and birds and lazing on the windowsill.

Our yard was her castle, and T. T. was queen of my heart. So I let her out. After all, T. T. always came back. But this time she didn't. By nightfall I was frantic. What if she'd been hit by a car?

"T. T.!" I called, my heart racing. The highway was only about thirty feet from our property.

Please help me find her, I prayed as I searched the neighborhood. *Where could she be?*

Despite my pleas to God, two weeks later there was still no sign of T. T. That Sunday it was my turn to teach the four- and five-year-olds in junior church. Still grieving the loss of my cat, I struggled to get through my lessons.

Get a grip on it, I thought. *It's only a cat. God's got a big to-do list. Why should He give two hoots about one lost fur ball?*

Nothing exceptional happened during the service until it came time for prayer.

"Okay, everybody," I instructed. "It's time to join hands in prayer."

Like little angels in a row, the children got up from their chairs and formed their familiar prayer circle.

"Who'd like to pray first?" I asked.

"Me!" said Daniel.

"Me next!" added Pattie as one by one they each began to pray.

"God, I need new runners. Fast ones. By Monday. Thank You. Amen."

"Dear Lord, my mommy is going to have a baby. Make it a girl. Thanks. Amen."

After a round of giggles and squirms, Donald caught me off guard when he asked, "What about you, Mrs. Knight? What do you need prayed for?"

Instantly voices started whispering in my head. *It's too late. T. T.'s gone. Don't tell these kids about your cat! You'll scare them.* Pushing doubts aside, I told them about T. T.

Little Katie began to pray. "Mrs. Knight's lost her cat. Please find T. T. for her. Amen."

"Today!" Donald added.

"T. T.'s gonna be there when you get home, Mrs. Knight," Pattie assured me.

"For sure!" Daniel said.

Their faith astonished me. I could see it in their smiling faces. They believed my cat was going to be waiting for me when I arrived home! I wanted to believe it. I needed to believe it. But I had my doubts.

Pulling into the driveway that day, I half expected to see T. T. come running to greet me. But she didn't. Still no cat. Sighing, I unlocked the back door and walked into the house. Plopping down on a chair, I let the tears come. At that very instant I heard a familiar meow.

Jumping up, I ran from room to room. "T. T.! Is that you? Where are you?"

Looking up, I spotted her. There she was sitting in her favorite windowsill, grooming herself and looking none the worse for the wear.

As I hurried to let her in, T. T. looked up at me as if to say, *Okay, what do you want to do first? Eat? Sleep? Play? Cuddle?*

Where she'd been for those two weeks, I'll never know. But this I do know: When a child prays, all of heaven listens. If you want to have a heart that beats with the certainty that God never runs out of miracles, one that believes unconditionally in the power of prayer, if you want to have a heart like Jesus, spend time with a child.

PASTRY BAG FAITH

Pat Butler

W e had forty-five minutes and one last errand to run before meeting my niece at the school bus. As the shopping center loomed on our right, my sister and I debated: Could we run the gauntlet of supermarket lines and get home in time?

"I can take Matt while you do your shopping," I offered. "I need only one thing."

My sister eyed me and then her son, calculating the risk of trusting an indulgent aunt with her six-year-old. "Okay," she decided, turning sharply into the parking lot. "But no fooling around! Thirty minutes—tops!"

We burst out of the van as soon as she parked and sprinted into the store. My sister disappeared into the crowd with her list; Matt and I headed for the kitchen gadgets. "Just need a pastry bag, Matt," I said.

Ten minutes later, after fighting through frenzied shoppers, finding the right aisle, and sorting through dozens of gadgets, I finally found the pastry-bag hook, dangling empty.

"Oh no!" I groaned as I envisioned my afternoon's baking plans evaporating. "Now what am I going to do?"

With the aplomb of a seasoned veteran of prayer, Matt replied, "You know what to do. You pray. You hold out your hands like this"—he held out both hands to take mine—"and you ask God and He gives you things."

Apparently my little talks and bedtime prayers with Matt had sunk in, but I had no faith to believe God would respond to an emergency request for a pastry bag. Surely He had more urgent prayer requests to attend to. As we bowed our heads, I first prayed silently, *Lord, I'm really sorry about this, but I need a pastry bag—*

"I know what to do!" I said as an idea as small as a mustard seed came to mind.

Grabbing Matt's hand, I rushed up the aisle with him. "Look for a store clerk!"

Matt bolted, flushed with the excitement of the chase. Any prayer that included running through supermarket aisles was his kind of prayer.

I glanced at my watch and began a second prayer. It would be as much a miracle to find a clerk as it would a pastry bag. I prepared my explanation of how God didn't always answer prayers the way we wanted when Matt's near collision with my sister at the end of the aisle interrupted me. She smelled trouble.

"Five-minute warning, you two!"

"Well, we have a problem…"

"Mom, we're praying!"

"Follow me!" my sister replied in response to my explanation. "I'll find you a pastry bag!"

"I know where they're *supposed* to be," I sighed, but I stopped as I saw her pulling a pastry bag from a second hook, a little further down the aisle.

"Matt!" I gasped. "Look! A pastry bag! God answered our prayer!"

Matt shrugged, smiling at my simplicity. My sister, ignoring my spiritual epiphany, herded us through the express line, back to the van, and home again, just in time for the school bus.

That night during our bedtime talk and prayers, I told Matt about the parable of the mustard seed. "Jesus said that if we had faith as small as a mustard seed, nothing would be impossible for us. And thanks to *your* faith, we got a pastry bag! I never thought we'd find one in time."

"How big is a mustard seed?" Matt asked.

"Smaller than a pastry bag," I answered, hugging him and thanking him for teaching me that God has enough time to manage *all* prayer requests, even emergency ones for pastry bags.

PRAYING FOR SNOW

C. Ellen Watts

It happens every time. The minute their parents announce plans for visiting Grandma and Grandpa, our California grandchildren come up with a dozen reasons why snow must be a part of their Idaho trip agenda. They also join forces and pray.

What those three fail to understand is that the snow they long for happens only once every seven or eight years. The snow for which they so earnestly pray falls on distant mountains—rarely in the southwestern part of the state where we live. Having been told all this, they remain adamant: If they pray for snow, they will get snow.

Each time our daughter and her husband choose to spend Christmas in Idaho, they realize that winter is not the wisest time to be traveling through mountains in a Chevrolet sedan without four-wheel drive. Donner Pass in the High Sierras is often closed due to heavy snowfall. The bleak mountainous stretches between Reno and McDermott, Nevada, can also be unfriendly. Once the family leaves Winnemucca and the freeway, driving the lonely stretch of two-lane that snakes across eastern Oregon to the Idaho border is often worst of all.

On one particular vacation, however, roads had been dry all the way. At the top of the last long hill, as the lights of a hundred farms and several small towns came into view, the parents turned to each other: So far so good. Despite the gloomy forecast heard on Boise's KTVB, God had held back the snow.

This fact did not gladden the children. Ten hours of steady driving, and not one child in the backseat had fallen asleep. While it was well past their bedtime and they could see that the landscape in every direction was void of snow, the children had not lost hope.

Sara, the oldest, spoke first. "Just wait. We're not there yet."

"It *always* snows at Grandma and Grandpa's," Katie said.

Jason, the middle child, was more outspoken. "You said it wouldn't snow last time, but it did."

"There will be plenty to do at Grandma's without snow," their dad said.

"You'll have your new Christmas things to play with—and your cousins," our daughter suggested.

Their dad made another point. "In order to snow, it has to be cold, and you know how you dislike being cold."

"*Snow* cold is different from regular cold," Sara said. "Besides, our cousins like snow."

Katie sighed. "I've been praying and praying."

That, our daughter and son-in-law realized from past experience, was a factor to consider.

Sure enough, halfway through the visit with us, the sky turned gray and it began to snow. Snow continued to fall the next day, though not enough to spoil the children's fun. The snow that fell was just right for kids to belly flop onto patched inner tubes and bounce down Simplot Hill. It was deep enough (after no small bit of shoveling) to make a snow cave beside Grandpa's driveway. And it was wet enough for snowballs and for building a snowman as tall as Mount Whitney—or so it seemed to three praying California grandkids.

Driving home over snow-slick roads meant slower traveling, which was no fun for the parents. But the kids were so happy and so filled with snow talk, the grownups found it impossible to be upset with them.

Our daughter and son-in-law heaved a sigh of relief as they left the last mile of slushy, gray pavement on the south side of the Sierras and stopped long enough to pull off sweatshirts. As heavier traffic announced their approach to Sacramento, it suddenly occurred to them that God had also heard their prayers. Snow for the kids; safe travel for all. The children were right. Jesus never fails.

The Trivial Prayer

JoAnn Reno Wray

t age four, our daughter, Amie, sent a determined prayer heavenward. God's answer forever changed our lives.

For months Amie had begged for a certain baby doll. Finally, on her birthday, the coveted doll arrived, a gift from doting grandparents. Amie named it Mandy and even beguiled me into crocheting "blankies" for it.

Weeks later, as I swept the garage, I heard Amie's cry from the playroom.

"Honey! What's wrong?" I called, sprinting inside to help.

She came running, her eyes filled with tears.

"Fix my baby, Mommy! Her head's broke," she sobbed. The doll lay in her arms, its head missing.

I examined the doll and asked Amie what happened to the head. Amie ran downstairs to get it.

The doll's head had been attached with an unbreakable plastic band reinforced with metal. Unable to repair it after working thirty minutes, I gave up.

Pulling Amie to my lap, I prayed for her, then added, "When Daddy gets home, maybe he can fix it."

"Really?" She sniffed.

"I can't promise, honey, but he'll try."

Burying her face in my shoulder, she wailed, "I want my baby fixed, Mommy!"

I rocked and comforted her until she dozed off, snuffling from time to time.

After my husband, Roger, came home, dinner and family activities filled the evening. Soon bath time arrived along with a tub of bubbles for Amie and her little brother, Mike. The sound of warm giggles filled the house.

Our little ones were soon ready for bed, and I tucked them in with kisses and a story. It was Roger's night for prayers, so he took over while I went to do dishes.

Later he joined me in the kitchen. He shook his head and said, "How did that doll lose its head? Do you know what she prayed?"

I'd forgotten about the doll. "What?"

Roger paused. "She prayed, 'Dear Jesus, please come down from heaven and heal my baby's head.'" He sighed. "What will we say if her prayer isn't answered?"

I shrugged. "Maybe she'll forget. Kids never stick with toys long."

"I don't know. She seemed very determined."

The next afternoon I was out in the garage again when I heard another cry from Amie. Before I could reach the door, she had hauled it open and galloped to me, extending her doll by its arms.

"He did it! Jesus came down from heaven and fixed my baby's head!" She danced around me, the doll mimicking her joyful bounce.

"Let me see!" I took the doll and turned it over and over. *Roger must have fixed it last night,* I decided. I grinned and swooped Amie up in a hug. "He sure did, honey! Praise God!"

She skipped off humming "Jesus Loves Me."

As soon as Roger walked in, Amie did an encore joy dance. "Look, Daddy! Jesus healed my baby!" Roger scrutinized her doll, then ruffled her hair. "That's great, sweetie!" He shot a questioning look at me.

Later, he finally voiced his question. "When and how in the world did you fix that doll?"

"Me? I thought you fixed it!" Stunned, we collapsed onto kitchen chairs. "You didn't?" I asked.

Roger shook his head. "Not me. I don't have the right tools or even know where to start. Was anyone else here today? Your dad?"

"Not another soul. Just me and the kids."

Roger gulped. "Then that means—"

"That Jesus came down from heaven and fixed Amie's doll." I finished his thought. "I sure didn't expect God to answer Amie's prayer," I added.

Roger nodded in agreement. "You and me both!"

We stared at each other, wondering how this could be. We discussed all logical possibilities. The doll definitely had been broken beyond our ability to repair it. And no one else had been in the house. Finally we concluded there was no other explanation except that God answered Amie's trusting prayer.

Never again have we considered anything too insignificant for prayer, and oh, the answers we've seen! From jobs supplied to finances met to our son Mike's miraculous healing from cancer years later. More than that, the answered prayers of seeing hearts of those we love reconciled to God.

All this joy because our daughter prayed with faith and determination for something her mom and dad thought too trivial to bother God with.

POTATO CHIP PRAYERS

Jean Hall

M y husband and I were Aunt Jean and Uncle Jerry to twenty-four children. We served in a home for abused and neglected children, who came to us through state authorities or because their parents voluntarily surrendered custody to us. Most of our children came out of fatherless households. Our home was part of a Christian organization dedicated to rescuing those children and raising them with love and godly principles. We taught the children to trust God, their heavenly Father, and to pray about *everything*.

Because we taught the children the value of work and responsibility, every child had a job to do every day. On one particular night, Christine and Laura had lunch-packing duty. Under Uncle Jerry's supervision they packed twenty-two school lunches for the next day. A sandwich, a piece of fruit, some cookies or crackers—whatever God had provided for us that week—went into the little brown sacks. The Christian school our children attended provided milk.

As Christine dropped Little Debbie cakes into the sacks, she said, "I'd sure like some potato chips. You know those little bags of chips. Everybody else at school brings them, and we *never* have them."

"Well, why don't you pray for them?" was Uncle Jerry's automatic response.

"Okay. I will."

That night we all gathered in the huge living room for family devotions. This was a sacred time in our home—nothing interfered with our time together reading God's Word and praying. We were conscientiously teaching our little ones to trust God and to pray about everything. We kept a running prayer list on poster board and faithfully checked off God's answers.

We worked our way around the circle of children taking prayer requests. They prayed for their parents, their pets, their school tests. The adults prayed for money for the electric bill and repairs on the van.

When it was time for Christine's request, she matter-of-factly asked God for lunch-sized bags of potato chips. All of us adults glanced sideways, silently communicating to each other, *Potato chips? Does she really think God has time for potato chips?*

The next afternoon, shortly after the children arrived home from school, a large truck pulled into our driveway. The bold red letters on the side read Lay's. Christine was in our dining room folding laundry and was one of the first to see the truck. She stood motionless, holding a towel in midair. She told us later that her heart jumped into her throat, and she thought, *Potato chips. God is sending me potato chips. Wow!*

Uncle Jerry greeted the driver as he climbed out of the truck. I was in the kitchen preparing dinner. *How nice. God is sending Christine a few bags of chips. Isn't it wonderful that He is mindful of a little child's prayers,* I thought.

I peeked at the chicken in the oven and stirred the green beans. When I glanced through the glass doors again, I saw six extra-large cardboard boxes stacked on the patio and Uncle Jerry and the driver shaking hands. Then the man climbed back into his truck and backed out of the driveway.

Meanwhile, Christine had left her laundry and was staring at those boxes. I was thinking, *Hmm, we can use plastic baggies and make our own little bags of chips for lunches.*

A couple of the older boys helped Uncle Jerry bring the six cases inside. We popped the flaps open to see dozens and dozens of little yellow and white lunch-sized bags of potato chips. Christine squealed and hugged everyone in the room. Uncle Jerry laughed with joy and praised the Lord. I stood silent, staring at the chips in disbelief.

When Christine had calmed down, Uncle Jerry explained. The driver had heard about our home and that we were supported strictly by gifts. His route had done poorly that week, and he had all those outdated chips to pick up from his stores. He asked if we could use them. If not, he would have to trash them. Uncle Jerry responded that we would be grateful for everything the driver could bring us, so please don't throw the chips away. Then the driver asked if he could stop by every few days to give us whatever he had to pick up from his stores. Uncle Jerry gladly accepted his offer.

The children, Uncle Jerry, and I stood in a little circle in the dining room and thanked God for His miraculous answer to Christine's potato chip prayer. We rejoiced over those chips as if they were the lost sheep coming home.

◄o►◄o►

Uncle Jerry and I stayed with that children's home for several years. For that entire time, each week, every week, that driver stopped by our home. Sometimes he brought lots of goodies; sometimes only a few. But Christine never again took a lunch bag to school without some kind of chips in it.

This all happened thirty years ago, but to this day, each time I rip open a little bag of chips, I recall Christine's potato chip prayer. We adults thought her request was cute but insignificant and undeserving of God's time and attention. But Christine had the kind of faith that believed Jesus meant exactly what He said: "If you believe, you will receive whatever you ask for in prayer" (Matthew 21:22). She assumed anything that was important to her, no matter how small, was important to her loving heavenly Father, the only father Christine had ever known.

Obviously, God agreed.

PART FIVE

"I HAVE HEARD HIS VOICE"

Children Trusting

Dear Jesus, please look after Daddy for my brother and me. We really miss him, but I know that he is happy there with You. The next time that You see my daddy, will You please tell him that I said "hi" and that I love him? Thanks, Jesus. I know I can depend on You.

—PAIGE, age seven

Please help put a hedge of safety around our family. Please help my slow burn and angry attitude when everyone is getting on my nerves.

—KEEGAN, age thirteen

Lord, help me not to have any bad dreams, and help my mom not to have any suggestions [he meant congestion] in the morning so she'll feel like going to church.

—CHRIS, age six

I wish I could trust like a child. I wish I could go to my heavenly Father in prayer, believing that my prayer would be heard and answered, just as a child knows that her mother or father will meet her needs. I want that kind of trust.

I'm not saying that parents give their children everything they ask for. Sometimes parents give their children exactly what they ask for, and sometimes parents say "no" or "wait" or "I have a better idea." But children trust that no matter what the answer, they have been heard, and they are loved.

Good parenting includes direction and protection. Children trust that their parents will say no when it is for their own good.

My son Barcley came to me once with a request to spend time with some kids I didn't think would be a positive influence. I wanted to say no but felt he needed some freedom to make his own decisions. Still, I was reluctant, and my hesitation was evident. I tried to buy some time but could only think of some trivial questions. Finally Barcley looked at me and said, "Dad, just say no."

I did.

Later I discovered that he really didn't want to spend time with these kids, but he didn't want to let that show. Instead, he came to me knowing (or at least hoping) that I would say no. He trusted that I would do what was in his best interest.

Parents are not perfect, but God is. God will always do what is best for us. We might think Him unkind or even cruel when He doesn't give us what we ask for. But just like kids who instinctively understand that God can be trusted, it helps to be reminded that whatever His answer might be, He loves us, He understands us, and He always cares for us.

—*Wayne*

FANNY CROSBY

Ethel Barrett

from Fanny Crosby

E *ditor's Note:* Blind from birth, Fanny Crosby went on to write over
nine thousand hymns, including "Blessed Assurance, Jesus Is Mine,"
"All the Way My Savior Leads Me," and "Redeemed, How I Love to Pro-
claim It."

In this excerpt from her life, a little background information might
prove helpful. First, in an earlier chapter of the book, the author tells us
about Fanny's pet lamb, Wooley, who had to be taken away because he
had become too dangerous. Second, Fanny and her mother have traveled
to New York City to have a surgeon examine Fanny's eyes. Dr. Mott was
"a great doctor," and Fanny and her mother have been praying that he'll
be able to restore Fanny's eyesight.

◄○►◄○►

Inside the doctors' office Mama takes a couple of steps and then falters
and stops. She leans over and whispers to me. "It's dark in here," she says.
"My eyes haven't gotten used to it yet." The nurse's starched apron swishes
as she leads us both through some double doors—the kind that slide
together—into a waiting room. There are several other patients in the
waiting room, but they're all grown-ups, Mama tells me. I am the only
child. It smells strange in here, like medicine. But there's something else
in the air.

"Why is everybody so afraid of Dr. Mott?" I whispered to Mama. She shooshes me and leans over close to my ear. She whispers that he is such a great doctor that everyone is in awe of him. They hang on his every word. They treat him as if he were some sort of a god. I listen for a while to the other patients talking. They speak in whispers as if they were on sacred ground. They talk as if they know each other and have been there many times before. They discuss Dr. Mott's and Dr. Delafield's marvelous feats of surgery. They use big words I can't understand. But I know I shall never forget them even if I don't know their meaning. I remember just about everything I ever hear, whether I understand what it means or not.

When it comes our turn to go in, a nurse and Mama both take my hands. I can't understand why they're both afraid of the two great doctors. The nurse introduces us.

I'm upset with Mama because her voice trembles as she says hello. But to me people are people and they either please me or they don't. I don't know whether they're great or not. Actually, the greatest man I know is my own grandpa. So I look up and smile to show that I like them and to show them how brave I am.

Dr. Mott takes me up on his lap. He tells me his name again and lets me feel his face. He has a short-cropped beard and a fine big nose. His eyes are deep-set and he has all his hair. I touch his hair lightly so I won't muss it. I can tell, both by his voice and by his face, that he is a kind, gentle man. Dr. Delafield comes close and holds his hand out for me to feel.

Then the doctors lift me up on the table. They start examining my eyes. They both talk softly to me all the while. Now, Fanny, this. And, now, Fanny, that. And, now, Fanny, we're going to do so-and-so. Don't be afraid.

And now I hold my breath waiting to hear what they will say as they begin to talk to Mama. They ask her questions and she answers with words like "poultices" and "drops" and they make little sounds down in their throats as she tells them how the doctor had treated my eyes for an infection when I was six weeks old. There is a little silence. We wait.

Then, "There is nothing we can do for this child's eyes," Dr. Mott says to my mother. "Malpractice has spoiled them—spoiled them for good."

He goes on explaining why this is so. But I don't hear. My mind has ground to a halt. After they finish talking they lift me from the table and set me back down on my feet. They pat my head and say things like, Poor little girl, and God bless you, and We're sorry.

Mama is crying softly. Both of the doctors and the nurse say nice things to her. She blows her nose. I do nothing. Maybe they think that I don't fully understand what they said. But I do understand.

It's just that there's one thought in my head and it's so big there isn't room for anything else.

It's hopeless.

I am blind for life.

I go through all the motions of shaking hands and saying my good-byes and thank yous. But the real me is down inside waiting until I can be alone with it. It is too terrible to share with anyone else.

-◄o►--◄o►-

I am lying on my bunk in the sloop. Except for different passengers, everything is just about the same. Captain Green is as kind and jolly as ever, so I don't let him know how I feel. Mama is so brokenhearted. I wouldn't dream of letting *her* know how I feel. I still think she thinks I don't fully understand yet and she's waiting until we get home to explain it to me better. But I do understand. I got it, every word of it. I know what *malpractice* means. And I know what *hopeless* means. Malpractice means the doctor did the wrong thing to my eyes and ruined them. And hopeless means forever.

I say good night to Mama and we stretch our arms out between our bunks and clasp hands and say our prayers. There are two of me now— the outside me and the inside me. The outside me says prayers with Mama and then we let go of each other's hands and roll over and go to sleep.

God, it's the inside me talking. I haven't been alone with you for a long time. In one way it seems like a long time—in another way it seems like only a few seconds. You already know it but I have to say it. I am blind for life. I am blind for life. No matter how many times I say it, it doesn't make sense.

God, the whole world is rushing by me. Everyone else is doing something important. Everyone else is going somewhere. My sisters and the other kids are going to school and they're learning to be doctors and carpenters and nurses and housewives and teachers.

God, I want to forgive that doctor. Then I want to put him out of my mind and never think about him again. I've asked you to give me my sight. I've asked you again and again. And I thought sure when we made this trip that you were going to do it.

I lie still for a while, thinking about what else I can say to God. I listen to the gentle slurp, slurp of the waves hitting the sloop. I pick up my thoughts.

...that you were going to do it, I say again. *I mind this. I mind it very much. There's no way I can be happy about it. But there's something else I mind a lot more.*

God, I haven't got a job to do. If you give me a job to do—I don't care what it is—I promise you that I will do it with all my heart.

I am quiet for a minute. Now the slurp, slurp is much louder than before. The waves seem to be singing to me. They seem to be telling me not to be discouraged. I sit up in my bunk to listen. They are singing! "Fanny, be brave! Fanny, be brave!"

I can scarcely believe this. My "inside" eyes open wide with amazement. I strain forward listening. The song goes on, "I have a job for you, Fanny. Brighter days are yet to come."

I sit up for a long time in wonder. I don't think I'll tell anybody about this, not for a while. Nobody would believe me.

◄○►◄○►

We've been home for a week now. For once I haven't talked much. But I'm not sulking, it's different.

Mama and Grandpa and Grandma—and even my sisters—know that something wonderful has happened to me. They don't ask any questions. They are all just relieved that I'm not sad.

Yesterday Mr. Drew stopped by our house. He's a drover—and he often goes by our house with herds of sheep and cattle. Anyhow, yesterday he stopped by our house and came up to the front porch. I was sitting in the swing with Mama and Grandma, helping them shell peas. They both "o-o-o-hed" as he came close to the swing.

"Hold out your arms, Fanny," Mr. Drew said. I did. And he placed something on my lap. It wiggled and squirmed and licked my hands. It was a very familiar feeling.

It was a baby lamb.

Grandma and Mama oh'd and ah'd and cooed with delight while I ran my hands gently over the little lamb's warm body. Then I lifted him back up to Mr. Drew. I told him he was very kind and I thanked him with all my heart.

"But I can't take him, Mr. Drew," I said. I tried to explain why. The only words that could come out were, "There can never be another Wooley."

I must have said it just right because I could feel that no one was angry with me. Surprised, yes. Angry, no. Everybody said more things after that—you know—polite things back and forth. And then Mr. Drew said good-bye and took the lamb back down to the road with him.

We went on shelling the peas in silence for a minute and then, "Some things can't happen more than once," I explained to Mama and Grandma. "This was my golden summer, and besides, I don't need a lamb anymore."

Well, that was a mouthful. And I suppose it will take them a while to try to sort out what I mean. But I know what I mean. And besides I know there are two of me now—an outside me and an inside me. And the inside me is in tune with God like it has never been before. And instead of feeling sorry for myself, I feel *special*, for the river waves have sung to me.

And I know that they are God's.

And that I have heard His voice.

BICYCLE PRAYERS

Ruth Bell Graham

from *Blessings for a Mother's Day*

E *ditor's Note:* When God answers prayer, sometimes He says yes, sometimes He says no, and sometimes He says wait. In Ruth Graham's story, her son Ned decides he wants a new bicycle, and he wants it now. He asks his father (Billy Graham, referred to as Bill), who tells him to wait. Even though Ned's request doesn't come in the way of a formal prayer, I've included this story because of its universal lesson.

───◄o►──◄o►───

Ned had reached the point in life when he wanted a bicycle more than anything. He had been playing with Joel Barker that fall, and he wanted one just like Joel's.

"Today!"

"No," Bill said. "Wait until Christmas."

And that was that.

So Joel lent Ned his new bike for a week. Before the week was over, Ned knew that Joel's bike would be too small for him in a few months. So he decided he needed a larger, ten-speed model.

The next week he saw one advertised in Sears with three speeds, stick shift, spring suspension, butterfly handles, triple brakes, slicks—the works!

This was the one he *had* to have (and it was still two months until Christmas)!

Then I understood, as never before, why God does not answer all of our prayers right away. Today we may be beseeching Him for things we would not want six months from now.

However, most of our prayers are not "bicycle prayers." When we pray according to God's will (that the prodigal may return; that the sorrowing may find His comfort; that He will work each situation out for our good and His glory), He hears us. For we know that each of these requests is what He wants.

But at times He has us wait for the answers.

The command "Wait on the Lord," found in Psalm 27:14, reads in the old Prayer Book Version (which is older than our *King James Version*): "O tarry thou in the Lord's leisure."

And to many of us impatient souls, how "leisurely" He seems at times!

Childhood Years

Kathleen White

from *Amy Carmichael*

I wish...oh how I wish!" Most children are familiar with the old fairy tale of three wishes that a foolish old man and his wife wasted due to their greed and stupidity. One little girl would have been well content with only a single wish granted. At three years of age, she was already old enough to have decided color preferences, and her greatest disappointment was that she had been born with brown eyes when she really longed for blue, to be like her mother.

From as far back as she could remember, her mother had impressed one thing on her: "Ask God, Amy, if you want anything badly. Share it with Him. He's never too far away to hear our prayers and He'll always give you an answer."

This seemed the ideal solution to Amy, so she knelt down and in simple childish faith begged God to change the color of her eyes.

So implicit was her trust in her Heavenly Father, she never doubted that the transformation would be effected by the morning. Upon waking, she climbed confidently out of bed and scrambled up to kneel on the seat of a chair she had pushed against the chest of drawers. Her eager, happy smile was reflected back at her from the mirror, but the eyes above the curving mouth remained a deep, dark brown.

Instead of feeling devastated because her hopes were not realized, her initial disappointment was replaced with the impression that God hadn't let her down after all. Neither had He failed to answer, just as her mother had promised. At that moment Amy dimly knew that "No" could also be an answer. God had surely heard, but sometimes He says "Wait" or "No" rather than an immediate "Yes."

What she couldn't appreciate at the time was what an asset those despised brown eyes would prove to be in the far-off future. God had a very good reason for saying "No" on that occasion. She had learned too a valuable lesson about Him, and she would be able to draw on that knowledge at other times of crisis and disappointments later on. Amy never underestimated the importance of that experience, and when she was older she wrote a poem about it, which was included in one of her books.

She need never have mentioned it again because it was only a fleeting, childish incident, but probably she decided to put it on record for posterity to help other children in their relationship with God. Perhaps they would understand better how He answered prayer when they had read a simple, real-life story. And children were what mattered most of all to Amy, right from the start. Years afterward, as she set off in search of poor, ill-used Temple children in India, Amy would stain her hands and arms and any other exposed area of skin with coffee, and put on an Indian sari so she could enter places where foreign women would be prohibited. Usually, she escaped detection, but had she possessed blue eyes she would have been recognized immediately as English. So God had a special purpose in creating little Amy just as she was, and she never tired of telling the Indian children in her care this story.

Words Worth Remembering

Patty Stump

O nly one week remained until the all-school spelling bee. Amid the daily disciplines of reading, writing, and arithmetic, Mr. G's fifth-grade class remained without class representatives for the upcoming competition.

With only a few days to go before the event, the time had come to tend to the task at hand. One by one the boys and girls made their way to the front of the classroom and nervously took their places in line. "Daniel, spell..., Grant..., Whitney..., Sara, would you please spell...." As Mr. G. made his way down the row of students, T. J. waited to take his turn. "T. J., would you spell...." T. J. carefully repeated the word he'd been asked to spell, pondered the sounds for a moment, and then uttered what he hoped was the correct spelling. Whew! So far so good.

Glancing down the row T. J. saw that a number of his classmates were still in the competition. Silently he wondered, *If I hurry, can I run to the bathroom and make it back before it's my turn again?* "Mr. G, may I please be excused?"

Quickly he raced out the door, down the hallway, past the water fountain, and into the boys' bathroom. Once alone, he took a deep breath and whispered a heartfelt prayer: "Lord, please help me to do well. I'd really like to be in the spelling bee."

Returning to the classroom T. J. was surprised to discover that only a handful of students remained standing. He resumed his place in line and clung to the hope that maybe this year he'd be a class representative for the event.

"John, spell…, Angela…, Austin…, T. J.…."

With each round that came and went, T. J. listened to the word placed before him, pondered it carefully, and then attempted to spell it with accuracy; each time relieved to have hit the mark. Finally, only five students remained standing, including T. J.

Round after round, word after word, the five contestants gave it their all, each successful in spelling the word given to them. With limited time remaining, Mr. G. announced, "Class, these five will be our spelling-bee representatives." T. J. was thrilled.

◄O►◄O►

As the school day came to a close, students darted from classrooms and bounded down the hallways, eager to catch a glimpse of their rides in the waiting line of cars. Racing toward our car, T. J. flung open the door, tossed his lunch box and backpack onto the backseat, and announced, "Guess what? I'm in the spelling bee!"

He couldn't wait to tell his sister as she climbed into the car, and he eagerly dialed his dad's cell phone to recap the victory with him.

After settling into the car and buckling his seat belt, T. J. turned and quietly shared with me, "I ran to the bathroom and prayed. I asked God to please let me be in the spelling bee." With a tone of disbelief, he said, as if to himself, "I can't believe it. I get to be in the spelling bee."

My heart whispered a prayer of thanks, for I was deeply grateful for the tender way my son had been encouraged and for the opportunity that lay before him. How delighted I was that he had looked to the Lord regarding his situation and that his tender faith had been strengthened.

The next afternoon I arrived at the school and took my place in the line of waiting cars. Three o'clock brought with it the familiar sounds of the dismissal bell followed by closing comments from the loudspeaker.

Students encumbered with backpacks engulfed the front lawn as they made their way to waiting vehicles. Scanning the activity for a glimpse of our son, I spotted T. J. slowly making his way along the winding sidewalk en route to our car. Something was weighing heavily on his mind.

Arriving at our car, he tossed his backpack onto the backseat, slipped quietly into the front seat, buckled his belt, and continued to glance downward. As we pulled out of the parking lot, T. J. choked back tears. With a lump in his throat, he muttered, "Now he says I'm not in the spelling bee. He'd written our names on the board and everything, but now he says he isn't finished picking class reps and that he has to start all over."

In the moments that followed, I listened as my son shared his disappointment. I struggled to make sense of it all and had little to say as we made our way home. Later that evening I called the teacher to find out more. Apparently the final selection of the class representatives would take into consideration additional information, such as test grades and overall averages.

When the process was completed, T. J. was not selected as a class representative for the annual spelling bee. He was deeply disappointed. As we talked through the situation, T. J. and I addressed the need to let go of what we didn't understand and still hang on to what we knew to be true.

Two Scripture passages helped add a renewed sense of perspective to the situation. From Romans 8:28, we focused on the fact that God's Word says He causes all things to work together for good and that while it may not seem to be so, nothing catches Him by surprise. He had heard T. J.'s heartfelt hope to be in the spelling bee, yet He had also chosen to move in a way that allowed those doors to be closed.

In light of this, a second passage offered truths that reminded us that even in the midst of disappointments and broken dreams, we do have choices—to trust God, to lean upon Him, and to release our dreams. Proverbs 3:5-6 states, "Trust in the LORD with all your heart and lean not on your own understanding; in all your ways acknowledge him, and he will make your paths straight."

Life lessons are the most common way we discover our daily need to simply trust.

The spelling bee came and went, and along with it, numerous opportunities for T. J. to lay before the Lord his heart, his hopes, and his hurts. T. J. has continued to discover that seemingly unanswered prayers touch each of our lives and are never easy to embrace. Yet amid the circumstances of everyday life, he has continued to cultivate a firmer foundation of faith—a realization that when all is said and done, the only thing we truly have to hang on to are the timeless truths of God's Word. For in them alone are we able to find the One whose words will never let us down.

"God Cut Me"

Karen Tenney Hitchcock

s we pulled up to the soccer fields, my son and I looked at each other. It was hard to tell which of us was more nervous.

He was the one trying out for the freshman soccer team, but I was the mother launching her firstborn into high school. Our school was large, well funded, and highly competitive. To survive there, a kid needed to find his niche.

Matt gulped. "Mom, can we pray?"

"Sure." I clasped his hand, and the two of us bowed our heads.

"Please, God," he pleaded, "help me make it on the team."

That prayer had been his summer litany, repeated over and over again at bedtime. And now the day had come for it to be answered. In my heart I was afraid of what a closed door might do to my son's fledgling faith.

He shouldered his bag, and I watched him trudge up the hill to the soccer field. "Thy will be done," I whispered.

When I picked him up at noon, his face was white. "I got cut," he said.

Neither of us knew it at the time, but that day marked the beginning of my son's greatest sports season—and so much more.

Being cut from the soccer team had immediate repercussions. Matt had signed up to play clarinet in the freshman concert band. Unless he could show he was involved in a fall sport, he would have to begin practicing with the marching band. For my sports-crazy son, marching band held about as much allure as water ballet.

Since soccer was no longer an option, football and cross-country were the only fall sports to choose from. It wasn't a difficult decision. Matt was five feet nine. Suited up for a game, even after a Thanksgiving dinner, he would still weigh barely 120 pounds. Football was obviously out. We'd heard a number of good things about the boys' cross-country coach, so we gave him a call. The coach was willing to take Matt, despite the fact that he'd missed most of their preseason conditioning.

That autumn I watched my son's life change. Matt's thin and wiry frame, such a disadvantage in other sports, was ideally suited to running. He surprised himself and everyone else by winning a fourth-place medal in his first race. The other runners were easygoing, intelligent, and humorous guys, and they instantly accepted Matt. That first week of high school, he was overwhelmed to actually be greeted in the hallways by upperclassmen. And since the team traditionally held pasta parties the night before each Saturday meet, he suddenly had a social life. Best of all, my husband and I had great respect for the man who was coaching our son.

God, however, saved the best for last.

I was home one September afternoon when Matt let himself in through the front door. He was sweaty and worn out from a practice run that had taken him farther than he'd intended. He asked if I would drive him back to the high school to pick up his books.

"Sure," I told him.

On the way we passed the soccer fields. "Hey, Matt," I said. "What do you know about the soccer team?"

"The freshman guys? They're pretty sad. All their best players moved up to junior varsity, so there's hardly anyone left who can score a goal."

"Ha," I said. "It sounds like they could have used you." I was still a little ticked because the team had refused to take my son.

"Maybe," he conceded, "But you didn't see the way I played at tryouts." He shook his head. "It was weird, like I couldn't buy a goal."

He paused, and I could almost see the wheels of his mind turning. "Mom! Can you believe it? It was *God* who cut me! He had to or I never would have found cross-country!"

I remembered that previous summer and how diligently Matt had prayed. In not receiving what he'd earnestly asked for, I'd feared his faith had been dealt a mortal blow. Instead, God proved to him that He'd been holding out for something better all along. Matt's prayer had simply been to make the team. In His wisdom, only God had known which team.

My son laughed. "Isn't it great? God cut me!"

JUMPING IN THE DEEP END

Patrick Borders

L auren, my six-year-old daughter, froze at the base of the diving-board ladder. My wife, Tonya, stood behind her. "Go for it, sweetheart."

I was treading water in the center of the deep end. "You'll be fine," I shouted to Lauren over the sounds of children splashing and laughing. "I'm here to catch you."

She stared at the board, her long brown hair blowing in the breeze. Waiting behind her, her younger brother, Jared, paced back and forth as water dripped off him onto the concrete. He'd already jumped once and had run back for a repeat performance.

Bands of sunlight reflected off the water and onto Lauren's face. Taking a deep breath, she climbed the rungs—pausing after each step. At the top she froze again.

An hour earlier, when Tonya and I picked up the kids from Vacation Bible School, Lauren had asked to go to the pool.

"I want to try jumping off the low dive," she said, smiling. "My Bible School teacher talked about Jesus giving us courage. She taught us the part from the Bible that says, 'I can do everything through him who gives me strength'" (Philippians 4:13).

The lesson had motivated Lauren to try something daring. Jared loved the pool; he knew no fear. But water intimidated Lauren; only weeks earlier she'd put her face under water for the first time.

I empathized with her. As a child, I had been afraid of the water. Even today the smell of chlorine can conjure up memories of my swimming instructor walking backward in the pool as I flailed my arms, struggling to swim to him. I wouldn't back away from Lauren; I'd hold her and protect her the second she landed in the water.

But I could tell her courage had fled. Her hazel eyes stared wide at the immense body of water surrounding her.

I held out my arms. "I'll grab you right away. There's nothing to worry about."

Sweat beaded on her forehead.

"Just jump to me," I said. "The water's nice and cool."

"No. I don't want to anymore."

"Come on, sweetheart. You can do it."

She stepped back and inched down the ladder.

As soon as she stepped away, Jared shimmied up and pranced out to the edge of the board. Without hesitation he leaped into the air and landed with a big splash. I grabbed him as soon as he came up and held his hand as we swam to the side. While Jared climbed out of the pool, Tonya walked quickly to me. "Look behind you."

I turned and squinted into the afternoon sun. The light embraced the clear silhouette of Lauren standing by the front edge of the board. She'd gone back up without anyone coaxing her.

I let go of the ladder to swim out to her.

"Wait," Tonya said. "Let's see what she does."

Lauren gazed down, apparently oblivious to us watching her. Her lips moved as if she was talking to herself.

She's trying to talk herself into it. My muscles tensed. I gripped the ladder, battling my urge to race out and catch her.

"Go for it, sweetheart," Tonya whispered. "You can do it."

Lauren's mouth stopped moving. She looked up. Slowly, she bent down and sprung high into the air, her arms stretched toward the sky.

Making a perfect cannonball, she grabbed her legs and splashed into the water.

White currents of water sprayed all around her.

She did it! I studied Lauren's image under water and waited for her to come up. Before I could swim out to her, she'd already turned and was swimming in my direction. She popped up ten feet from the side and swam the rest of the way on her own.

"Way to go!" Tonya cheered. "I knew you could do it!"

I wrapped my arms around her when she arrived at the ladder. "That was awesome!"

Lauren beamed. "I remembered what I learned today. I can do everything through Jesus. I kept praying that Jesus would give me strength." Lauren grabbed the ladder rails. "I knew if I jumped, He'd take care of me."

She bounced up the ladder and strutted off to take another turn—a new pro at jumping off the diving board. For the next hour she stayed in the deep end, trying to leap higher and higher from the board.

As I watched from the side, I realized that life will only bring more deep waters for Lauren to jump into—ballet performances, school tests, college, marriage—and I won't always be there to catch her. But Jesus will always be with her. And as long as she relies on Him, she'll have the strength to take a leap of faith.

PART SIX

"DEAR JESUS, WE NEED A DADDY"

Children Asking

Jesus, please come into my heart. I have trouble being good, and I could use your help. Thanks!

   —SAMUEL, age six

Dear Lord, help my cat…he died.

   —KATE, age five

Dear Lord, help me and Scott not to argue. Help Mom not to get frustrated or angry. Help us to work extra hard. Help me to be a good example to our neighbors. Thank You for this day. Thank You for our breakfast. Help our lunch and dinner to be good. Amen.

   —SEAN, age eleven

God, please help my Mommy and Daddy. They take showers together.

   —VICTORIA, age five

K ids are good at asking for what they want. Perhaps a little too good. When my children were young, taking them to the mall was challenging. Everything their little eyes saw, they had to have. New games, new shoes, new clothes, whatever was on the shelf, they had to have it, and they didn't hesitate to ask.

Somewhere between childhood and adulthood, many people have lost the art of asking. Perhaps we have forgotten that our heavenly Father wants us to bring our requests to Him. Ask. I didn't give my kids everything they asked for, but I tried to say yes more often than no.

Our heavenly Father encourages us to ask. As the requests from the kids in this book demonstrate, nothing is too small—or too large—to ask God for. He doesn't always give us everything we ask for, but He always gives us everything we need. It's just that we have a perception problem.

I am reminded of the story Dr. James Dobson shares in his book *Stories of the Heart and Home* about a little girl who wrapped an empty box and gave it to her father as a gift. When the dad discovered the box was empty, he was angry with her for wasting paper and asked why she had wrapped a box with nothing in it. She replied that the box wasn't empty. She had filled it with her love and kisses. She stood there and blew each kiss into the box and put her love in there too.

Perception. We need to remember that God doesn't always give us the things we want. Sometimes His gifts are even more special than the thing we asked for.

—Wayne

BIBLES, BAPTISM, CERTIFICATES, AND OTHER SIGNS OF CHURCH LIFE

Beth Moore

from *Feathers from My Nest*

O ne of the dearest of all my church memories is the baptism of each of my children. Amanda was six years old when she announced, "Guess what, Mommy! I asked Jesus into my heart!" I was caught totally off guard. "When did you do such a thing?" I asked. I had always pictured how I would be the one to pray with my children to receive Christ. "Last night in my own bed. It was just me and Jesus. Is that not OK?" I pulled my silly self together and said, "Of course it is, sweetheart. Of course it is. Just tell me all about it." I was convinced she understood her decision, but I felt that we should wait until she was a little older to be baptized. I wanted her to remember it forever. I suggested that if she felt the same way when she turned seven, we would progress toward public baptism. Many months passed. The morning of her seventh birthday, I was awakened by her tender little voice whispering in my ear, "He's still in there." It was so precious. She was baptized a short time later.

Keith and I were so proud. *Melissa was furious.* She knew that at our church a person could take the Lord's Supper if she had received Christ and followed His example with believer's baptism. Just before the next ordinance, Melissa announced, "I am asking Jesus into my heart." She was only five. "You are? Honey, that's wonderful! What has brought you to such an important decision?" Her response nearly slew me, but I had to push the hold button on my laughter and save it for later: "Because I'm as hungry as anybody at church." Needless to say, we waited a while.

Melissa grew up considerably over those next two years and decided there was more to receiving Christ than eating in church. She looked like an angel in the baptistry. I was scared to death she'd take the opportunity to address the church body while she had their attention, but, thankfully, she resisted. She did, however, maintain a keen interest in the Lord's Supper, asking me repeatedly when the next occasion would be. She hated for her big sister to get to do *anything* before she did, and she had waited several long years. Finally the weekend arrived.

To my heart's dismay, she developed a stomach virus Saturday night. I finally got her to sleep around 2:00 A.M. A few hours later I crawled out of bed and whispered to Keith, "I need you to stay home with Lissy if you don't mind. She can't possibly go to church, and I've got a class to teach. Is that OK?"

He responded astutely, "Am I going to be the lucky one to tell her she's not going to church to take the Lord's Supper today?"

I retorted, "That's the plan." We both chuckled.

My plan backfired, however, when Melissa caught me sneaking out the door. She looked so sick and her face was dreadfully pale. Still, she yelled, "Mom! You can't leave without me! I'm taking the Lord's Supper today."

My heart just broke. "Baby, you have been sick all night. Not only that, you are terribly contagious. I am so, so sorry, but you can't possibly go today."

She burst into tears. Her next words are etched in my memory forever: "Then can you just get it *to go?*" I suddenly pictured a drive-through window at my church and one of our pastors handing out a white paper bag. I nearly died. She was so sincere that I had to push the hold button again and save it for later.

Needless to say, we didn't get the Lord's Supper *to go*. But I did borrow some little cups from my church, run by the grocery store, and get just the right kind of grape juice and crackers. That afternoon, we had our own little worship service. We sang, read the Scriptures, prayed, then partook of the Lord's table right there in our den. God didn't mind. We felt His presence there in the middle of us. To this day, it is one of the most precious memories of an ordinance that I have stored in this feeble mind of mine.

As special as our home-style worship service was, we didn't make a rule out of observing the ordinances at home. The next Sunday, we were right back in our places, taking part in corporate study and worship. You see, the home was never meant to replace the church any more than the church was meant to replace the home. Even in the "home churches" that congregate around the world, the two influences are distinct. Home and church were meant to complement one another…and help one another out. Christ was raised in a home *and* a house of corporate worship. He still has an affinity for showing up at both. When He drops by the church, may He find choir teachers kneeling, children singing, seekers studying, and worshipers worshiping. Some things you just can't get "to go."

◄○►◄○►

Editor's Note: I chose to include Melissa's story because she demonstrates the childlike quality of hungering and thirsting for the things of God. Even though the story isn't strictly about prayer, it still models for us the kind of desire that God longs to see in His children. Wouldn't it be great if we could go to God in prayer with the same measure of desire that Melissa demonstrated? After all, we get hungry too.

INNOCENT PETITIONS

Robin Jones Gunn

from *Night Light for Parents*

When we lived in Nevada, my daughter Rachel had a best friend named Kristin. We moved to Portland, Oregon, only a few days before Rachel's first day of second grade. Each night we talked about her new school and prayed together before she went to bed.

The night before school started, Rachel prayed that Jesus would give her a new best friend at this school and that her name would be Kristin. I felt compelled to alter her prayer but decided to let it go. How do I tell my child she shouldn't be so specific with God?

The next morning, Rachel stood in front of the mirror while I combed her hair. She seemed lost in thought, and then suddenly she announced to me that Jesus was going to give her a new best friend. Her name would be Kristin, and she would have brown hair, just like the Kristin in Nevada.

I quickly ran through all my mental notes on prayer. What would be the best way to explain to this child that prayer is not telling God what we have in mind for Him to do, but rather seeking His mind? I tried a few flimsy sentences. All fell flat. She seemed undaunted. I drove her to school, still unable to find a way to protect her from her own prayer. I was afraid she would experience a spiritual crisis when she arrived at school and found no brunet Kristin in her class. What would that do to her innocent faith?

We entered the classroom, and Rachel found her name on her new desk. She lifted the top and began to examine the contents. I sat down at the desk next to hers and decided this would be a good time to explain how praying isn't like wishing. It's not magic. You can't ask God for something and expect it to materialize at your command. She needed to be willing to accept whatever new friends God brought to her.

I was about to plunge in, when out of the corner of my eye I noticed the name of the student who would occupy the desk next to Rachel. There, in bold black letters, was printed *Kristin.*

I could barely speak. "Rachel," I finally managed in a whisper, "look! There *is* a Kristin in your class. And she's going to sit right next to you!"

"I know, Mom. She's the one I prayed for."

The bell rang, and I practically staggered to the back of the classroom as the students began to come in. Rachel sat up straight, folded her hands on her desk, and grinned confidently.

I glued my eyes to that door. Four boys entered. Then a girl with blond hair who took a seat in the front row. Two more boys and then, there she was! She sauntered shyly to the "Kristin" desk, caught Rachel's welcoming grin, and returned the same.

I probably don't need to mention that she had brown hair—down to her waist.

Or that everything I really needed to know about prayer I learned in second grade.

THE PROBLEM

Gigi Graham

from *Weatherproof Your Heart*

> Your attitude should be the same as
> that of Christ Jesus.
> —PHILIPPIANS 2:5

I stood in the upstairs hallway, looking down over the bannister, waiting for the younger children to come in for their baths. My oldest daughter, taking a piano lesson, was in the living room directly below, and the repetitive melody she was playing echoed through my mind. Standing there, I savored both the few moments of solitude and the aroma from the roast beef and apple pie already in the oven.

Suddenly the little ones bounded through the door. I cringed as I saw their muddy footprints on the white carpet and their filthy little hands leaving distinct imprints on the cream-colored walls. They bounced up to their rooms, cheeks flushed and eyes bright from their play.

I noticed, however, that one of my young sons was trudging slowly up the stairs, his head bowed, grubby hands covering his small, dirt-streaked face. When he reached the top, I asked him what was wrong.

"Aw, nothing," he replied.

"Then why are you holding your face in your hands?"

"Oh, I was just praying."

Quite curious now, I asked what he was praying about.

"I can't tell you," he insisted, "because if I do, you'll be mad."

After much persuasion I convinced him he could confide in me and that, whatever he told me, I would not get mad. So he explained that he was praying about a problem he had with his mind.

"A problem with your mind?" I asked, now more curious than ever. What kind of problem could a six-year-old have with his mind?

"Well," he said, "you see, every time I pass by the living room, I see my piano teacher, and my tongue sticks out."

Hard as it was to keep a straight face, I took his problem seriously and assured him that God could, indeed, help him with it.

Later, on my knees beside the bathtub as I bathed this little fellow, I thought how I still struggle with the problem of controlling my mind and my tongue. All too often my mind focuses on the negative until negativism dominates my thoughts and actions. I find myself being critical and unpleasant. Repeatedly I realize that I have said what I didn't mean to say, and haven't said what I really wanted to say—such as, "Thank you" or, "Well done!" or even, "I love you." All too often I focus on faults, while ignoring or forgetting the much-needed word of praise, encouragement, or appreciation.

That afternoon as I knelt to scrub that sturdy little body, the tub became my altar; the bathroom, my temple. I bowed my head, covered my face, and acknowledged that I, like my son, had a problem with my mind and tongue. I asked the Lord to forgive me and to give me more and more the mind and heart of Christ.

WANTED: A FRIEND

Lynn Schwander

My seven-year-old son, Jeremy, adopted Teddy Ham just in the nick of time. The four-ounce fur ball of a hamster took Jeremy's mind off the bully at school.

Routinely Jeremy was teased and came home upset. "The bully called me rotten redhead today," Jeremy sobbed. "And he pushed me into the girls' bathroom. He threatened all of my friends."

I contacted the principal and documented the boy's aggressive behavior. But I prayed nightly and often cried myself to sleep after tucking my freckle-faced son into bed.

One afternoon my son exclaimed, "The bully told the entire class that 'shrimpy Jeremy wet his pants, and he smells.'"

Fighting back my tears, I asked Jeremy if he wanted to pray for a best friend—one that would help him through this difficult time.

He nodded eagerly.

"Dear God," he prayed, "bless me with a friend."

"Send a buddy with courage," I added. "A friend who will stand by Jeremy even when others are mean."

"Amen," we said.

Determined to cheer Jeremy up, I asked if he wanted to go somewhere special—a happy place.

"The pet store," Jeremy replied without hesitation, and his face brightened.

Later that day I caught a whiff of sawdust mixed with fish-flavored cat food when I opened the pet shop's front door. Birds cawed, puppies whined, and aquariums bubbled. Jeremy walked down each aisle looking at the reptiles and bunnies. Then he stopped at the rodent section.

A teddy-bear hamster scurried across the cage. Jeremy touched his finger against the glass. The furry, brown rodent with white patches followed Jeremy's index finger inquisitively. Jeremy bent down and gazed into the creature's eyes before it scampered back to its nest.

"Can I have a hamster, Mom?" Jeremy asked, his eyes pleading.

"If you want to take Teddy Ham home, you have to promise to talk to him quietly and hold him gently," the shopkeeper said. "You're not buying a hamster; you're adopting a new family member—one that takes a lot of effort. We call him Teddy, but you won't know for about two months whether he's a boy."

After Jeremy promised to carefully handle the animal and I handed over a hundred-plus dollars for hamster paraphernalia, we drove Teddy home.

Teddy wasn't the most considerate household member. The nocturnal critter's exercise wheel squeaked at all hours, keeping the rest of the family from sleeping. Frequently the small, fluffy animal's plastic activity ball ricocheted off the furniture and walls while Teddy hurried inside the sphere, racing through our home. Occasionally our entire family crawled around on hands and knees looking for the tiny escape artist. But the sparkle that returned to Jeremy's eyes when he found Teddy made it all worthwhile.

I wanted to dress Teddy in a red cape and shirt with an *S* on it. He (or she) was my hero, a wonderful distraction for Jeremy.

About two months after Teddy arrived, we had concluded that he was a boy. For some reason that reminded me of our prayers that God would send Jeremy a special friend, so I asked him if he had found someone yet.

"Maybe," my son answered.

"Then maybe you can invite him over," I replied. "By the way, how're things at school?"

"Fine, the bully still says things, but I ignore him." Jeremy picked up Teddy. "Teacher said I can bring my critter for show and tell tomorrow." Teddy wriggled his nose and squirmed in Jeremy's hands.

The next day I carried Teddy and his cage into Jeremy's second-grade class. The room filled with *oohs* and *aahs*. I eyed the room, looking for the special friend.

When Jeremy took his turn for show and tell, hands rose immediately.

"What does he eat?" a girl dressed in pink asked.

Could she be the brave soul? I wondered.

"Can I hold him?" a blond boy begged.

He's a possibility, I thought.

Even the bully quizzed Jeremy on hamster trivia.

Before the teacher dismissed the class for lunch, I caught up with Jeremy and whispered in his ear, "Good job. Which one is your special friend?"

"It's Teddy." Jeremy looked at me puzzled. "You didn't know? Isn't it funny, Mom?" My son grabbed his lunch box and took his place in line.

Yes, isn't it funny? I thought, *God doesn't always answer the way we mothers imagine. And isn't it funny that it takes a child to point out the miracle taking place before our eyes?*

Jeremy waved. The bully trailed behind him, yelling out, "Hey, Jer, do you think you could tell me more about hamsters at recess?"

"Hey, God," I whispered, "Do you think You and Jeremy can teach me a little more about prayer?"

"WE NEED A DADDY"

Marilyn Martyn McAuley

During lunch four-year-old David laid his fork firmly on the table and said, "Mother, when are you going to get us a daddy?" The fact that he called me *Mother* told me the degree of importance his question held. Mommy was my usual title.

I glanced at three-year-old John, whose large blue eyes were fixed on me waiting to hear my reply. I wondered for a moment how I should answer, because I hadn't intended to remarry. Nine months earlier cancer had claimed their father's life, and I didn't want to risk marrying someone who couldn't or wouldn't love my boys the way they needed to be loved. Finally I said, "Well, boys, I don't know of any available daddies, so I guess we better ask Jesus to help us. Okay?"

They both nodded and resumed eating. But they did not forget my promise to ask Jesus for a daddy.

That evening the boys, all clean and smelling sweet from their baths and snuggled in their soft sleepers, knelt down at the side of the bed with me and prayed. John was first. "Dear Jesus, please give us a daddy. Amen."

Then David prayed, "Dear Jesus, we need a daddy. Will You find a daddy for us? I love You, Jesus. Amen."

I hugged them to me as I prayed, also asking Jesus to give us a daddy who would love us and take care of us.

The boys were happy as I tucked them into bed. They acted as if a burden had been lifted from their small shoulders. They trusted Jesus to answer their prayers.

Once they were asleep, I knelt beside the bed again and poured out my concerns and needs to God. I loved my boys dearly and wanted the best for them. If they needed a daddy, then I wanted one for them, but I also needed to protect them. What to do?

Finally I relinquished my decision to remain single. Though I had faith that God would provide just the right man, I still asked for certain qualifications. First, he must be a godly man, and second, I hoped he would be a teacher.

The three of us continued praying nightly. A month and a half later, just a few days before New Year's Eve, two of the apartment owners knocked at our door. They were brothers in partnership with their father. I worried that a tenant had complained about the boys running down the hall.

"Hi, I'm Bruce, and this is my brother, Dan." We shook hands, and Bruce said, "We're painting the apartments and would like to begin with this one. Is it convenient for you if we come next Saturday?"

"Yes, I'd love to have it painted!"

That Saturday I let the boys go to their friend's house to play. As Dan rolled fresh paint on the walls, he began talking. I learned that he was a godly man who loved children, which is why he became a teacher. Bit by bit I began to realize that he might be the daddy the boys and I were praying for. Before the day was over and the painting was done, he asked, "Have the boys ever seen the ocean?"

"No, they haven't."

"Every child needs to see the ocean. May I take you and the boys to the beach tomorrow?"

"We would love to do that. Would you mind joining us for church first?"

"Not a problem. I'll pick you up for church, and then we'll get a bite to eat before we head for the beach."

When David and John came home, I told them about Dan and that he would be taking us to see the ocean tomorrow after church. They were two excited little brothers. But kneeling to pray at bedtime, we continued to ask Jesus for a daddy.

That Sunday was wonderful. All of us hit it off right away. After that, Saturdays became family dates. I loved watching the boys' faces light up when Dan came over. John started calling him Daddy on our second date. He believed that Jesus had answered our prayers.

Eventually I also became convinced, and on Memorial Day weekend, forty years ago, we walked down the aisle to become a complete family with both a mommy and a daddy.

Today the boys are not only fathers themselves, but grandfathers, too. David said recently that this was still the most wonderful answer to prayer he has ever had. The boys learned at an early age that Jesus cares about their problems, and it strengthened my faith to place our future completely in God's hands. We still love His provision for us.

KELSEY'S PRAYER

Lanita Bradley Boyd

K elsey, our lively daughter who brings great joy to our lives, is also quite the independent thinker. As a young girl she frequently got into trouble by doing things I would never have thought of, such as walking the length of a seesaw or cutting the pictures out of a book to paste into her own book.

So I worried about how she would do in school. I could imagine that instead of writing her name on her paper, she would draw vines and flowers down the sides, and it would be the prettiest paper, but not necessarily what the teacher wanted. As a teacher in the school she attended, I walked the halls warily her first week of first grade, wondering if her teacher, and my friend, Barb Yaksic would indicate that she needed to have a little talk with me. But Barb simply smiled and said, "That Kelsey is a doll!" so I gathered that all was well.

Friends and relatives asked Kelsey how she liked school.

"It's okay," she answered.

I assumed her lack of enthusiasm came from being more restricted than she liked to be.

Toward the end of the third week of school, we assembled as usual for family prayers before bedtime. She and her fourteen-year-old brother, Josh, were willing participants. Sometimes their prayers were more obligatory than thoughtful, but occasionally we were astonished at their depth.

When it was Kelsey's turn to pray, she mentioned the relatives she always prayed for, and then softly added, "And please make Mrs. Yaksic like me." The catch in her voice kept her from going further, and I went ahead with my part of the praying.

After Kelsey was in bed, her dad and I went in to kiss her and tuck her in, another nightly ritual. I sat on the side of the bed and asked, "What's going on with you and Mrs. Yaksic?"

That was all she needed. Between gasping sobs, she told how miserable she had been in her first-grade class. Mrs. Yaksic hugged everyone else, but not Kelsey—at least not often. Mrs. Yaksic was always giving special help to some children, but never to Kelsey. "She's not mean to me. She just doesn't seem to like me," Kelsey ended.

As a teacher I thought I understood what had happened. I had been totally wrong in my expectations of Kelsey. Perhaps she was such a good and reliable student that Barb was leaving her on her own while she dealt with the new first graders who had bigger problems.

Gently, I told Kelsey that that was the way I saw it. "I'm sure she'll pay more attention to you when she gets some of the problem children settled," I assured her. "Remember to keep praying about it. That's always a good move."

Her situation pestered my thoughts as we rushed to get ready for school the next morning. I kept praying for something to happen that day that would reassure Kelsey and establish a more comfortable place for her in the classroom.

"Lord," I prayed, "please help Kelsey adjust to the situation. Help Barb sense her needs and meet them as much as possible." Immediately I felt a sense of peace. I knew that somehow God would work it out.

As I opened my plan book at school, my eyes fell on the schoolwide schedule of special classes, and I knew what I had to do. I checked it to find out when Barb would be in the classroom while her students were out.

After she had time to walk her class to the gym and return, I quietly eased into Barb's room. As I silently prayed that I would use the right words, we chatted for a minute. Finally I said, "What kind of problems are you having with Kelsey?"

"Problems?" she repeated. "Absolutely none! She's well behaved and does her work beautifully. Why do you ask?"

I told her. Shaking her head, she slowly sank into her chair.

"I am so glad you told me this!" she responded. "I had no idea I'd been ignoring her. Well, that's a problem easily remedied. Thank you so much for telling me."

After school Kelsey burst into my classroom. "Mom! Guess what! I got to be Mrs. Yaksic's special helper today! She asked me to put books on the shelf for her, and she said I did a great job. I *love* Mrs. Yaksic!"

"Great!" I answered, hugging her. "I guess those prayers paid off pretty quickly."

She stopped short. "Oh yeah! I forgot all about that. I guess it was those prayers. I didn't quit praying last night until I went to sleep. I prayed all the way to school too."

"So did I," I answered. "It's a good thing God doesn't forget children's prayers." *And that He prods mothers in the right direction,* I thought. *Keep prodding me, Lord, to be the mother You want me to be. Help me to ask the right questions and to depend on You for the answers.*

TREY'S PRAYER

Dorothy Hill

One of the biggest fears any parent can have is being stranded on the side of the road at night with a small child. Does the parent stay put in the car and hope that someone will stop, or do the parent and the child begin walking to find help? With the hope of aid comes the fear that someone, the wrong one, will stop.

That was the dilemma Susie and her seven-year-old son, Trey, faced when their car broke down in a deserted spot one evening. Cell phones were not commonplace at that time.

"Momma, do you want me to go for help?" Trey asked. "I'm not so little anymore, you know."

"You are my right-hand man," she answered, "but I think I'd feel much better if you stayed here with me."

"I won't let anything happen to you." He patted her shoulder.

"And I pray that nothing happens to you," she said, trying to keep her fears from spreading to him.

The approach of headlights brought both relief and panic. The mixed feelings intensified as the car passed without stopping.

"Tell me again about your day," Susie said.

"But I've already told you everything, twice." There was a skittish sound to his voice that he couldn't hide from his mother.

"I know, but I like to hear about what you are doing," she said in an effort to calm him. "You're my son, and I love you. What is important to you is important to me."

"Do you think Daddy will look for us?"

"I'm sure he will." *If he knew we were in trouble. If he knew where to look.* She could go on and on with the ifs if she allowed herself, but that wouldn't help the situation.

"Lord, we need Your help," Susie began to pray aloud. Why hadn't she thought of this sooner? She reproached herself as she prayed for God's protective arm to be around them in that dark, secluded spot. Her husband might not know where she and Trey were, but God did. He could send any number of angels to protect them.

Trey joined his mother in prayer as he, too, asked God to send someone to their aid. But the child wasn't taking any chances. He wanted help from more than invisible angels. He wanted someone with skin on. "Please send Jeff Cunningham to help us," he added.

Oh no, Susie thought. Her grown-up wisdom told her what her son's inexperience did not. Their former neighbor was a highway patrolman, but this was not his assigned area. Right now he should be at home with his wife and son. How could she explain that Jeff would not be coming without damaging her son's tender faith?

At the sight of approaching headlights, she pulled her son closer. Panic began to set in when she realized the car was slowing down. When the car came to a stop, Susie quickly sent up another flare prayer for God's protection.

Suddenly blue lights began twirling. As the other car's door opened, the interior lights came on and revealed the face of Jeff Cunningham. God had answered Trey's prayer.

Susie never asked why Jeff was on that road that night. It did not matter. What was important to her was the level of faith her young son had shown in the emergency when he made a specific request. God had responded by sending Jeff. Why had she thought that this was beyond His control? Where was her trust?

Parents don't often admit that they learned a lesson, especially a faith lesson, from their children, but Susie does. She learned from her son's trusting prayer that God not only listens to prayers that go beyond the generic "help me" to the specific "send Jeff," but He also answers them.

PART SEVEN

"Do I Haf to Tell You What I Done?"

Children Praying Honestly

I pray that I would have the strength to avoid getting frustrated with my two annoying brothers that torment me daily. Help them not be so grumpy and crabby all the time.

—LAUREN, age eleven

Lord, I know You love them, too, but could You p-l-e-a-s-e help my team win the ball game?

—WES, age ten

Help me to not always want the biggest piece of cake. Help me to watch my tongue.

—ELIZABETH, age seven

Dear God, I've been trying to kick a football. Why haven't You been helping me?

—JORDAN, age nine

As a teenager I was active in my church's youth group and was involved in a ministry team that led services on Sunday mornings. One hot summer Saturday evening found our group scheduled to lead worship in an unfamiliar church twenty miles from home. The local pastor invited us to his house that afternoon for some snacks and leisure time. Following that, our driver took us to the pastor's church so we could practice the songs we would perform the next day.

My turn in the speaking rotation had come around, and I was to deliver the message on Sunday morning. I asked if I could remain behind at the church after practice so I could study my sermon. The pastor's house, where I was to spend the night, was near the church, and since I'd been there earlier, I felt confident I knew how to return.

I was wrong.

After I finished my preparations, I strolled in the direction of the minister's home. Darkness had already changed the contour of the land and my memory. In a matter of minutes, I was lost and frightened.

I tried retracing my steps in an effort to start fresh, but the disorientation prevented me from finding my way back. As the darkness and fear overwhelmed me, the intensity of my prayers grew. Not only was I afraid of wandering the streets, but I was even more terrified of being attacked by strangers.

In my desperate situation, I questioned the very existence and power of God. I begged God to help me find my way, but heaven was as dark and quiet as the night.

Finally, realizing that I was hopelessly lost, I prayed, "God, if You are God and if You care about me at all, please help me. I'm going to hitchhike. Please send me someone to help. Don't let me get hurt. If You can't do this one simple little request, then I don't believe in You."

The prayer was honest. The time had arrived in my life to test the waters. I needed to know for myself if God did, in fact, hear and answer prayers.

A pickup truck approached. I stuck out my thumb. The driver pulled over, and I got in. I explained my situation and gave him the minister's name. He drove straight to his home and let me off.

I asked God for a ride, and I got one.

That experience taught me that it is okay to be deeply honest with God. He can handle our doubts, our anger, our disappointments, and our fears.

Children are honest with God, and they remind us that we can be too.

—*Wayne*

DISOWNED DESIRE

John Eldredge

from The Journey of Desire

A young woman came to see me, as most seeking counseling do, because she was at the end of her rope. What had begun a year earlier as mild depression had sunk deeper and deeper until she found herself contemplating suicide. We met for many weeks, and I came to know a delightful woman with a poet's heart, whose soul was buried beneath years not so much of tragedy but of neglect. This one particular afternoon, we had spoken for more than an hour of how deeply she longed for love, how almost completely ignored and misunderstood she felt her entire life. It was a tender, honest, and deeply moving session. As our time drew to a close, I asked her if she would pray with me. I could hardly believe what came next. She assumed a rather bland, religious tone to her voice and said something to the effect of "God, thank you for being here. Show me what I ought to do." I found myself speechless. *You've got to be kidding me,* I thought. *That's not how you feel at all. I know your heart's true cry. You are far more desperate than that.*

I wish she'd prayed like my son Luke. He is our youngest son and very wise for all of his five years. He knows what he wants and what it means to lose it. "My life is over." Luke laid his head down on the table and sighed, a picture of lament. I had just told him he couldn't have chocolate-covered sugar bombs for breakfast, and he was devastated. There was no longer any reason to go on. Life as he knew it was over. I enjoy Luke because he has more undisguised and unadulterated desire than anyone I know. He is "out there" with his desire and his disappointments. When we go over to someone's house for dinner, the first thing he'll ask will always be, "Is there dessert?" Part of me has tried to train this out of him; part of me admires the fact that he isn't embarrassed by his desire, like the rest of us. He is unashamed. We hide our true desire and call it maturity. Jesus is not impressed. He points to the less sophisticated attitude of a child as a better way to live.

THE DAY BART SIMPSON PRAYED

Lee Strobel

from *What Jesus Would Say*

B art wasn't doing very well in the fourth grade. When he flunked his book report on *Treasure Island* because he knew only what was on the cover, that was the last straw. His teacher called a meeting with Bart's parents and the school psychologist, whose conclusion was that Bart should repeat the fourth grade.

Bart was horrified! "Look at my eyes," he said. "See the sincerity? See the conviction? See the fear? I swear I'll do better!" After all, nothing's worse to a ten-year-old than being held back in school.

Then Bart hatched a plan. He made a deal with a brainy student named Martin. He'd teach Martin how to be cool if Martin would help him pass his next American history exam. That final test was monumentally important because if he passed it, Bart would be allowed to graduate.

Bart did teach Martin the fine points of being cool—how to burp on command, spray-paint graffiti on garage doors, and shoot a slingshot at unsuspecting girls. And, sure enough, Martin became the most popular student in school—so popular, in fact, that he didn't have time to help Bart study!

Now picture this: It was the night before the big test. Bart was sitting at the desk in his room, staring at an open book, trying to study, when he came to the chilling realization that it was too late. He couldn't cram enough into his head in one night to be able to pass the test. Finally, his mom peeked into the room and said, "It's past your bedtime, Bart."

Slowly, Bart closed his book. With the exam just hours away, it seemed like all his options had evaporated. That's when he got down on his knees next to his bed and prayed to God.

"This is hopeless!" he said. "Well, Old Timer, I guess this is the end of the road. I know I haven't been a good kid, but if I have to go to school tomorrow, I'll fail the test and be held back. I just need one more day to study, Lord. I need Your help! A teacher strike, a power failure, a blizzard—anything that will cancel school tomorrow. I know it's asking a lot, but if anyone can do it, You can. Thanking You in advance, your pal, Bart Simpson."

The scene switched to an outside view of Bart's house. The lights in his room went out. It was cold and dark. A few moments passed, and then a single snowflake gently fell to the ground. Then another. And another. Suddenly there was a virtual avalanche of snow; in fact, it was the biggest blizzard in the city's history! The *Hallelujah Chorus* swelled in the background.

The next day school was canceled. Bart fought the temptation to go sledding with his friends and instead studied hard. Then the following day, when the time finally came for the test, he gave it his best shot. Even so, he came up one point short. It looked like he had failed—until, at the last possible moment, he miraculously scored one extra-credit point and squeaked by with a D-minus.

Bart was so happy that he kissed his teacher as he scampered out the door. Homer was so overwhelmed that he posted Bart's paper on the refrigerator and declared, "I'm proud of you, boy."

To which Bart replied: "Thanks, Dad. But part of this D-minus belongs to God."

What Bart Did Right

Isn't that great? If Bart were a *real* boy and he prayed a *real* prayer like that, I think Jesus would say, "Bart, there are four major things you did right. Let's talk about them. The first thing you did right was this: You prayed directly from your heart."

One recent survey showed that while talking to God is a nearly universal activity among Americans, more than one-third of them merely recite formula prayers when they communicate with Him.

But Bart didn't just repeat some fancy language he had learned in Sunday school. He didn't try to lower his voice two octaves. He talked to God directly from his heart, pouring out his frustrations and fears.

Why did he feel so free to do that? One reason is that he was alone with God at the time. The Bible says in Matthew 6:6, "When you pray, go into your room, close the door and pray to your Father, who is unseen. Then your Father, who sees what is done in secret, will reward you."

That makes sense, doesn't it? If I have something very intimate I want to say to my wife, Leslie, I don't want to say it in front of others, even if they're friends. I wait until Leslie and I are alone.

Now, there's nothing wrong with group prayer, public prayer, or praying with your spouse. Those can be quite appropriate and beneficial. But there's no substitute for regular, one-on-one, heart-to-heart talks between just you and God—when you're not trying to impress anybody else with your spirituality, put a positive spin on a bad situation, or hold anything back.

Are you creating those opportunities for yourself? For Christians who are deeply involved in church, it's easy to feel that the praying they do in ministry settings is enough. But it's not. We all need to get alone with

God—whether it's in the morning, during lunch, or at night—so we can feel the uninhibited freedom to be vulnerable and honest with Him.

If necessary, do what I've done on occasion: In the midst of busy periods, when I'm most susceptible to forgetting to connect with God, I make an "appointment" with Him in my daily schedule. I actually write in, "12:30: Meet with God." That way I make sure I've set aside some time for a heart-to-heart talk.

THE FLAT TIRE

Tony Campolo

from *Let Me Tell You a Story*

W henever I think about the work of the Holy Spirit, I immediately think about what my friends in the Vineyard churches call "signs and wonders." Indeed, there are signs and wonders all around us, and more things are happening that ought to be called miraculous than we are ready to affirm.

THE POWER OF MIRACLES

I, myself, can attest to one miracle that defies any talk of natural explanation. When I was in high school, our family was very, very poor. I took a number of odd jobs trying to help out my parents.

One day, I discovered there was a large bakery just a few blocks from our house that at the end of the day made bread available for sale at one-tenth the regular price. I quickly figured out that there were a couple of diners around who would buy that bread from me at triple the price I paid for it. And so I became an entrepreneur. At nine o'clock at night I would go to the bakery, buy a pile of bread, put it in a wagon that was tied to the rear of my bike, deliver it to the diners, and sell it.

The miracle happened one night after I had delivered all the bread and was on my way home. By then, it was about eleven o'clock. There was a freezing drizzle in the air that soaked my coat and made my body shiver.

I don't remember a night being any darker or colder than that one seemed to be, and as I tried to make my way home I felt nothing but misery. Then, all of a sudden, the tire of my bicycle blew out. I had one of those old Schwinn bikes with balloon tires, and when a tire blew it did it with a bang. It's hard to describe what I thought and felt at that moment. I got off my bike, sat down on the curb, put my head in my hands, and started to cry. I was tired and I was beaten. I had tried so hard to be a good boy and earn some money for my family, and then this had to happen. I remember moaning, "God, everybody thinks You're good, and maybe You are to other people, but it seems like You're mean to me. How could You let this happen? Why can't You help me? You know what? I think after today, I'm just not going to believe in You anymore!"

I don't know how long I sat there, but eventually I got up and started to push my bicycle on what I knew would be a long trek home in the freezing rain. I hadn't gone very far when I noticed a gasoline station. I don't know what made me do it, but I went over to the air pump in the station and tried to put some air in the blown-out tire. Usually those pumps are turned off at the end of the day, and there was no air to be had when the compressor wasn't working. If I had stopped to think about it, I would have known how futile it was to try to put air in that tire. It was blown out—bad! But I tried. I put the nozzle from the air pump onto the valve of my tire and pulled the lever that releases the air. Incredibly, air flowed! The tire inflated! I couldn't believe it.

I didn't hesitate. I climbed on my bike and pedaled home in the dark, saying over and over again, "Thank You, Jesus! Thank You, Jesus! Thank You, Jesus!"

When I got to my house, I carried my bicycle up onto the front porch and locked it up. It was then about eleven-thirty. I put the key into the lock of the front door, and just as I was about to turn it, there was a sudden swishing sound. I turned around and watched as all the air left the tire. Within seconds, the blown-out tire was completely flat again.

In the morning, when I went to look at the tire, I saw there was a rip on the side of it that was at least three inches long. The inner tube was torn apart. I knew that something miraculous had happened!

Looking back on that evening, I honestly believe that God looked down and saw a kid who had been pushed just as far as he could go. I was on the edge and He wasn't willing to allow me to be pushed beyond that which I was able to bear. The Bible promises that God intervenes in such situations (1 Cor. 10:13). I have a feeling that I just might have given up on the whole Christian thing if God hadn't stepped in with a miracle at that point. But He did!

A Double Dose of Lessons

Laurie Barker Copeland

I s there really a God?" asked thirteen-year-old Kailey who became a Christian at the age of four. I, like Kailey, accepted Christ as my Savior at an early age, but it wasn't until I was thirteen that I made that decision with the full knowledge of what it meant. Now *my* thirteen-year-old was asking the same questions I had. She wasn't mad at God, nor did she doubt His existence because things weren't going her way. She simply wanted to make Him *her* God, and not her parents'.

She confessed her doubts to her dad and me, and the three of us discussed them openly. John and I then prayed that God would make Himself known to her in a personal way.

A couple of months later, Kailey, in her usual teenage tornado-like mode, left shirts, hair bands, and wet towels everywhere as she got ready for our church's youth group. In addition to leaving the mess, she talked back to me. The flippant attitude and messy room were problems we had been dealing with for quite awhile.

After Kailey left, I took stock of her attitude and the destruction she had left behind. I reminded myself to discipline her when she returned, but by morning, I realized I hadn't dealt my daughter's punishment.

As I sat there letting the sleep drain from my head, I was overwhelmed with the thought, *Forgive her. Forgive her for everything. Furthermore, call her in the bedroom and tell her you are forgiving her for everything.*

This was not my usual mode of operation. Everything I knew about child rearing told me to be consistent with discipline. Let them know who is boss. Let them know they can't get away with misbehavior. All good points. *If this is God's prompting,* I wondered, *would He want me to be inconsistent and let her get away with misbehaving?*

This "total forgiving" idea did not make sense to me, but I knew within my spirit that I needed to extend grace to Kailey. Calling her into the room, I explained that I was forgiving the bad behavior from the day before. Smiling, I said, "I know you are a good girl with a heart for God, and I love and appreciate you."

She looked at me shocked, her blue eyes welling with tears. She looked at her father and asked, "Did you tell her?"

"No," said my husband in astonishment.

"On the way home from youth group last night, I told Daddy I wished you would appreciate my good points more often and not always come down so hard on the things I do wrong. Daddy suggested I pray about it."

Before she went to bed the night before, Kailey prayed, *Dear God, I pray my mom sees me as someone who tries. I may not always get everything right, but I'm trying. Help her to see that, and to remember the good things I do.*

Kailey sat before me with tears running down her sweet face; then a small smile began to form. She was humbled and happy. That was the beginning of her journey in understanding what it feels like to be a child of God. God hasn't always answered her prayers in the way she's wanted. But just when she needed it, He gave her the assurance not only of His existence but also of His power.

We discovered a double dose of lessons that day. Kailey not only had her prayer answered, but I learned to listen for God's prompting—that still, small voice that told me to go against reason. Without it, I might have missed the glorious opportunity to be involved in a young girl's answered prayer.

A Loving Reminder

Anita Higman

When I was eleven, talking to God made me anxious. At times I wondered if a wish made on a shooting star would rise up to the heavens just as effectively as prayers to an invisible Creator. As a Christian I did pray, but in some hidden nook of my heart, I didn't know for certain if He would bother with the whimpering pleas of a misfit like me, especially when it came to the trivial stuff that made up daily school life.

But like a parent giving a reassuring hug, God had a loving reminder for me, which came through a remarkable event. During my sixth-grade year, an announcement was made to our class that we would be creating a show for the whole school that would offer samplings of various types of dance from different countries.

All sixth-graders were expected to perform in the show, and no one in my class had a problem with the request. Except me. My family attended a church that didn't approve of that particular extracurricular activity, and I knew I would be the only one who wouldn't get to participate in the performance. A few kids might have secretly counted that restriction a blessing, especially the more timid ones in our class. But not me. I loved all things related to the arts, and the idea of not being able to be in any part of the program left me deeply disappointed as well as embarrassed.

What would I do? I decided to pray about it. Simply, but with great sincerity, I sent my request to the Lord. How would He deal with the situation? And why would He care, anyway? Wasn't He too busy keeping wars at bay?

Very soon after my petition to heaven, my teacher called me up to her desk and said, "I've been thinking, and I believe you'd be perfect as Uncle Sam in our production."

I was stunned by what my teacher said because, first of all, I would be a girl playing Uncle Sam, and second, my teacher wasn't aware of my dilemma. Uncle Sam was to be the MC of the show, the only role that would not perform any of the dances. With great relief, I immediately agreed.

My heart shouted heavenward, *Wow, God, You actually care about me. Even a kid who questions You from time to time!* When the performance time finally came, I wore a festive red, white, and blue Uncle Sam costume and had a great time being the MC of the program.

Since those days long ago, my denominational views on dancing have altered some, but I realized that wasn't what I needed to focus on. God had given my heart a gentle reminder that prayer wasn't like the fantasy of wishing on a shooting star. Prayer was a powerful and intimate way not only to present my needs to God but to communicate with my Creator. I admit my childhood prayer didn't move any mountains, but it certainly moved my world that day. God had watched over my comings and goings and cared for me far more than I could ever care for myself.

An Honest Heart

Diane H. Pitts

T he sunlight bounced off the white linen tablecloth in Emma
Mitchell's breakfast room. We sipped hot tea and watched our children catapult off the jungle gym to the trampoline. Something was always
happening at the Mitchell home, so I wondered what catastrophe or comedy Emma would paint for me today.

Almost as if reading my mind, Emma narrowed her dark eyes and
asked, "Did I tell you what Robert did last week?" Four-year-old Robert
Mitchell was a one-man mischief machine even without his twin sister,
Sarah. Today Robert stood center stage during our teatime conversation.

"The bird nest was right outside on the front porch, close enough for
us to watch the birds building every day. Robert watched the mother bird
guard the three eggs," Emma recalled. "I can't tell you how many times I
told those children not to touch them; I made that *perfectly* clear."

Emma gazed out the windows at the figures bursting into view—Elle,
Will, and the twins, Robert and Sarah. My boys joined the mix as well.

"The children kept watching until the eggs finally hatched." Emma
continued the story, remembering a particular morning Robert sidled up
beside her as she put the finishing touches on cinnamon rolls.

"Mama, de burds are soooo cute!" Luminous chocolate eyes blinked
with every word. "I touched dem; I reawy did. They are so soft."

"Right. Soft birds... You couldn't have touched them, Robert. They're
too high for you."

Robert mumbled to himself, "But dey're so cute...and soft!"

The warning lights in Emma's head blinked only in the distance, her mind filled with other things. Robert walked dejectedly from the kitchen as Emma called her husband, Ed, to come down for breakfast.

Five minutes later four different voices yelled outside the window. The front door slammed, rattling the pictures in the foyer. From the landing on the staircase, Ed scanned the four troubled faces below.

"Okay, what's the problem?" he asked.

A chorus erupted.

"Daddy, they wouldn't fly!"

"We were only trying to help 'em!"

"Now they won't move."

"Daddy, the mommy bird is *so* upset!"

Characteristically, Ed took matters in hand. "Show me," he directed.

The children piled through the front door with Ed close behind. The porch boards creaked with each footfall, then silence. Ed looked down the front-porch steps to the grassy lawn, his eyes pausing at three small mounds of feathers. Eight fearful eyes glanced from their father to the devilish handiwork. A distraught mother bird swooped in and out of nearby trees.

Anger swept over Ed's face and then melted away as quickly as it had come. He pulled the children out to face him and squatted down to their eye level.

"The tiny birds are dead. It wasn't time for them to be out of the nest." His tone softened. "Do you see how sad and frightened the mother is?" He sighed. "Now you are going to have to bury the little birds."

Before breakfast, with shovels in hand, the Mitchell foursome buried their dead. They went about their task with grief-filled eyes and sagging shoulders. Random sniffs and stifled sobs could be heard all the way into the kitchen, where Emma quietly prayed for her erring children until the job was completed.

Later, during family devotions, Emma sensed a true sorrow on the part of everyone, except Robert. Usually quite tender-hearted, he didn't comment about the birds. When time came for his prayers, the words sounded hollow.

"Thank you for this day and for our rolls. Bless Sweet Mama and Jim. Bless Hanna and Bill…" The list rolled on but with no regret for a deed committed. After the final prayers were uttered, Ed and Emma went straight to the heart of the matter, talking with Robert after the other children ran outside to play.

Emma began to pray, "O God, we are so sorry that the baby birds died. Robert didn't mean to get them out of the nest. The others made bad choices too by not stopping him."

First a quiet sniffle, then one tear after another coursed down Robert's cheeks; his heart began to thaw. Instinctively, Ed and Emma pulled Robert close. His little raspy voice piped up, "God, do I *haf* to tell You what I done?" He peeked toward his parents. Seeing their nods, he continued. "Okay. Let me tell You what happened."

And Robert Mitchell came clean before the Creator of boys and birds, telling Him about everything. When he vigorously pronounced the final amen, his eyes shone with fresh forgiveness. Ed and Emma hugged him, sent him outside to join the others, and breathed a sigh of relief.

Concluding the tale, Emma looked at me over the teacups. "His prayer was really honest—from the heart. You know, I really need to write down all the things I learn from these children."

As she rolled on to another topic, I could only nod. I mulled over Robert's prayer. Finally honest. A gentle nudging began in the corner of my mind, causing my heart to churn as I wrestled with my thoughts. *God already knows the truth, yet I cover it with shallow words and stifle the obvious.*

When will I learn to confess right away and keep communication unbroken with God? He knows my thoughts before I think them and where I am going before I even start out. He just wants me to have an honest heart like Robert's.

PART EIGHT

"WOULD YOU PLEASE HEAL MY GRANDPA?"

Children Persisting

"Dear God, please help my brother be good and not tell lies," the five-year-old prayed.

"I don't tell lies," the eight-year-old cried, giving his brother a hearty punch to the shoulder.

"You do too. And dear God, help him do what Mama tells him to."

"What do you mean? I always do what Mama tells me."

"Don't interrupt my prayer. Dear God, please help my brother do his homework when Mama tells him to."

"I did my homework."

"Dear God, please make my brother stop interrupting when I'm saying my prayer."

"I'm not interrupting you."

"See, God. He did it again."

—TUCKER, age five (pray-er) and PARKER, age eight (interrupt-er)

One childhood memory I easily recall is traveling eight hours in a 1960 Buick LeSabre from Cincinnati, Ohio, to Big Stone Gap, Virginia. Our summer vacations always included a trip to Big Stone Gap to see our grandparents, aunts, uncles, and cousins. During the course of the trip, the one question that was asked more often than "Can we stop at Dog Patch?" was "Are we there yet?" I asked it, my older brother, Randy, asked it, and my younger brother, Walter, asked it.

Children have a built-in persistence that aggravates parents. Consider this story by Rick Warren:

> What do you want for Christmas this year? If you were to ask a typical little boy, he'd give you two words: *Power Rangers.* There's a little boy I know named Brian. For weeks he bugged his parents about getting a watch for Christmas. Finally his dad told him, "Brian, if you mention that watch again, you're not going to get it. Quit bugging us!"
>
> One night Brian's parents asked him to lead in prayer before dinner.
>
> Brian said, "I'd like to quote a Scripture verse before I pray. Mark 13:37: 'I say unto you what I have already told you before—watch....'"
>
> Now that is appropriate use of Scripture!*

Indeed, not only is it a good use of Scripture, it's also a good model for persisting in prayer.

In Luke 11, Jesus tells a story about a man who needs bread to feed

---

an unexpected guest. He goes to a neighbor at midnight, wakes him, and asks for bread. At first he is told to go away because the hour is late and everyone is in bed. But because of the man's persistence, the neighbor gets up, gives him what he wants, and sends him on his way.

The man is rewarded because he refuses to take no for an answer. I don't understand the reasons why Jesus would want us to seek, and keep seeking, until we find, but He does.

Following Jesus's teaching and taking a cue from Brian, I am encouraged to take my petitions to God and to continue to ask until I get an answer, even if it means finding creative ways to make my requests known.

I bet Brian got his watch.

—Wayne

ONE RING

Phil Callaway

Ask my eldest child, Stephen, which J. R. R. Tolkien work is his favorite, and he won't skip a beat. Ask him about a moment when his prayers seemed silly, and he just might grin.

His favorite books by a country mile are the Lord of the Rings series. To my utter amazement he had read all three of the thick tomes by the age of ten. Before we celebrated his fifteenth birthday, he had read them three times and had started them a fourth time.

Crazy, I thought. He read them between playing basketball and ice hockey and table tennis. He read them in the evenings when he should have been studying. He read them late at night when he should have been snoring.

When he learned that director Peter Jackson was bringing the stories to life on film, I had to peel him off the ceiling. From beginning to end my son can tell you more than you want to know about Middle Earth, about hobbits and goblins, about the "One ring to rule them all." The filmmakers should have used him as a consultant.

Shortly after we viewed the first *Rings* movie together, Stephen turned sixteen. It was the time in life when fathers and sons have whispered conversations about life and love and being grown up. One night during one of those discussions, I spoke to him of the importance of reaching this milestone. How, like his favorite hobbit, Frodo, he would be faced with great temptations and great opportunities as he journeyed through the darkness of this earth. I said I would like to present him with a small gift as a covenant between him and me that he would walk the way Frodo had walked, choosing to do the right thing, though it cost him everything. I talked of putting God first. Of faith. Of purity. He nodded his approval.

"What's the gift?" he asked. When I told him, he smiled widely.

The next day I ordered it.

On the evening it arrived, we assembled for a family ceremony. The children gathered around wide-eyed as I opened a wooden box. Inside was a genuine, rather expensive replica of the ring. White silver, complete with elfish engravings.

"Where's ours?" said the other two children.

"You wait," I told them.

I read a short verse of Scripture: "So honor the LORD and serve him wholeheartedly" (Joshua 24:14, NLT). "For sixteen years that's been our prayer for you, Stephen. That you would honor God and serve Him."

We prayed together, committing this child and his future to God. Then I took the ring, hung it from a gold chain, placed it around his neck, and kissed his forehead before he squirmed away.

There the ring stayed—until the night Stephen arrived home from school carrying small pieces of the chain. He could scarcely bring himself to tell me.

It had broken, he knew not when. The ring was gone, we knew not where.

We searched everywhere. Along sidewalks and hallways. Through classrooms and in cars. Nothing. It was permanently gone, I knew. Hanging around someone else's neck. Adorning another's jewelry case.

But Stephen began to pray.

His younger sister and brother joined him too. At suppertime they prayed that we would find the ring. At breakfast they prayed believing. I hated to doubt, but I am a grownup. Doubting is what I do best. I knew that if the ring was found, it would be kept by the finder. And the odds of that finder residing in our family were rather slim.

"There's more chance of the Chicago Cubs winning the World Series," I told my wife.

"They're not even in it," she said.

"Precisely."

Months passed. Winter came and went. The snow that covered the field through which my son sometimes walks to school began to melt.

One evening as we sat down to eat together, I noticed a particularly wide grin on his face. As we dived into some roasted chicken, he told us he'd been walking home from school when a glint of reflected sunlight caught his eye.

Then he held his hand out and opened it. I couldn't believe my eyes. The ring. White silver with elfish etchings. As good as new.

Oh me of little faith.

I had prayed that my son wouldn't be too disappointed when his prayers weren't answered. He had asked God to do the impossible, something God has delighted in doing since the dawn of time.

The ring hangs around his neck from a sturdier chain now. I hope it will remind my son to honor the Lord and serve Him wholeheartedly. I hope it will remind him that those who seek find, that those who ask receive. May he never stop believing in the God of the impossible.

BLACK SHOES AND CHRISTMAS

Cecil Murphey

Our commander announced a dress inspection for Saturday, four days before Christmas vacations began. My shoes, barely acceptable for daily duty, wouldn't stand up under inspection. I needed a pair of black, navy-regulation shoes.

In transferring me to Great Lakes, Illinois, six weeks before Christmas, the navy had lost my pay records and allotted me ten dollars a month for incidentals. (It would be February before they realized that they had been spelling my name incorrectly.) I didn't know anyone well enough to borrow money. My commander wouldn't let me out of the inspection, even though I volunteered for extra duty. *What am I going to do?* I asked myself repeatedly.

Late Thursday night, in desperation, I walked into the dimly lit chapel and sat in the last row. For a long time I tried to form prayers that refused to come.

Then I remembered a time in childhood when I had needed a pair of shoes. Two days before Christmas, Mom still hadn't said anything about our presents. At the sink I soaped a plate and rinsed it.

"Elmer's getting a dog for Christmas."

Instead of taking the plate from me, Mom shook her head slowly. She didn't look at me, but even at nine years of age, I sensed that something wasn't right. Before I could ask what was wrong, she removed her glasses and polished them with the bottom of her apron.

"We won't have any Christmas this year," she said.

"Dad's working again," I said. He had been sick for two months but had gone back to work after Thanksgiving.

"There...isn't...any...money." She burst into tears and buried her head in her apron. Dad's first check had gone for rent, groceries, and gas for his car.

Mom picked up her purse, fumbled inside the money section, and emptied its contents on the kitchen table. A dime and three pennies rolled across the checkered oilcloth.

"That's all the money until after Christmas when your dad gets paid again."

"God will give us what we ask for," I said. "See, Mrs. Garbie [my Sunday-school teacher] says we should pray."

"I...have...prayed," she said as fresh tears came.

The answer seemed simple to me. "Mom, you have to tell God *exactly* what you want, then you'll get what you ask for."

"Sometimes we don't get what we want."

"My teacher said we would, and she knows. So you'd better make a list and pray."

She tried to smile as she pulled a pencil stub from her purse and sharpened it with a paring knife. On the back of a calendar she wrote our names and listed a toy for each of my two brothers.

"Now what do you want?"

"New shoes," I said. Even at that age, I was the practical kid in the family. The sole of my brown shoes had come loose on the right foot, and I had finally cut it off. By the next day I had worn a hole through the innersole and my socks as well. I stuck pieces of cardboard into the bottom, but they wore through after I walked in the snow.

"And I want black ones."

"What if you get something else?"

"No, I'm going to get black ones."

Our school principal wore black shoes with metal taps on the heels. When he walked down the hallway, I liked to listen to the clicking of his heels. I didn't know anybody whose shoes shined so brightly. I wanted a pair the same color.

"I'm going to ask for black, and that's what God will give me. Mrs. Garbie said so."

I didn't know much about praying, but I told God about the principal's black shoes and that I wanted a pair like his.

"They don't have to be that nice," I said. "I just need shoes. And God, just to be sure You know, I want to tell You again: I want *black*."

When Christmas morning came, we all gathered in the living room as soon as we finished our oatmeal. We didn't have a tree, but Mom had hung red and green strips of crepe paper over the windows. Her eyes brimming with tears, she handed my two younger brothers and me a small bag of candy. Then she began to sing "Silent Night." When she was sad, she often sang hymns.

My dad didn't say anything. He kept his head down while he tied and retied his shoes.

Just then a Salvation Army truck pulled up in front of our house. My brother Mel ran to the door. He brought a fat, smiling man into our living room, who handed Dad three large boxes.

"We didn't ask for help," Mom said.

"Somebody told us," he said. At the door he smiled again and said, "Maybe it was God."

"It was!" I yelled. "God told them!"

My brothers had fun pulling out boxes and trying to figure out who they were for. I waited for my shoes. Mel handed me a box of checkers, but I wasn't much interested; I only wanted my shoes.

Soon the boxes were empty. "Where are my shoes?"

"I guess there aren't any," Mom said.

"I asked for black shoes. Why didn't I get them?"

I couldn't cry in front of my dad, so I stomped my foot.

"Sometimes God just doesn't give us—"

"Maybe He took them to the wrong house."

Tears stung my eyes, but I wasn't going to give in.

"Everything doesn't work out the way we want," Mom said, stroking my shoulder.

"God promised!"

As far as I was concerned, I had done what Mrs. Garbie told me, and God hadn't kept His promise. I had been so certain about the shoes, and now I didn't know what to do.

"I'll wait," I said. "Maybe the truck will come back soon."

No matter how often I ran to the window and looked outside, the Salvation Army truck didn't come back. No one else brought gifts.

Mom cooked a Christmas dinner of chicken, cranberries, and sweet potatoes from the food they gave us. I didn't want food; I just wanted my shoes. Every time I heard a car, I hurried to the window.

Finally, just before dark, I walked to the end of our snow-covered street to see my friend Chuck. Since I wasn't going to get my shoes, I didn't want to be home where I'd keep thinking about them.

Each year for Christmas, Chuck's father bought rebuilt shoes for the family—shoes brought in for repair and never claimed. I went into their house and took off my shoes because my feet were cold and my right foot was soaking wet. I rubbed my toes to get them warm again.

"Look," his mother said and pointed to my shoes.

"I didn't mean to make a mess," I said, embarrassed about my tracks on her linoleum floor.

Mr. and Mrs. Baldwin whispered something to each other, and Mrs. Baldwin went into another room. When she came out, she handed me a pair of shoes.

"If you can wear them, they're yours," she said.

I stared at them. They were black! Although rebuilt, they had been polished so nicely, they looked new. I held them up to my face and smelled the polish.

"They'll fit all right!"

Those were *my* shoes, and I knew it.

"We got them for Chuck, but they're too small," she said, "and the man won't take them back." She said Chuck could wear his brother's shoes from the previous year.

My left foot slid right in. I put a cold, wet right foot into the other. I tied the shoes, stood up, and walked around. They were a perfect fit, just as I knew they would be.

Minutes later I raced into our house. "Look, Mom! God gave me the shoes after all!"

Mom looked up and smiled. It was the brightest smile I'd seen on her face in months. Tears followed her smile.

I walked around the room to show off my shoes.

"See, just what I asked for. And God even gave me the right color."

Thirteen years later I remembered that incident when I needed shoes again. But I had long since lost faith in the God of my childhood. However, in a search for meaning in my life, I had begun to attend church again. In the chapel I asked God in awkward sentences for a pair of black shoes before Saturday.

On Friday when I came back from lunch, someone had put a brown bag on my desk. I opened it, and inside I saw a pair of navy-regulation black shoes.

I pulled them out and stroked the new leather. Someone had polished the tips to a bright glow. Several members of the personnel section where I worked beamed at me. Although I hadn't said much, they knew about my lost pay records. One of the guys gave me a thumbs-up.

I grabbed the shoes and hurried into the head (the men's room). I put on the shoes—just my size—and tears flooded my eyes.

I stared at the shoes' reflection in the mirror and thought, *Twice God has provided shoes when I needed them. And not just any shoes, but black ones both times—just what I asked for.*

From the gift of black shoes, I learned a valuable lesson. If I could trust God to provide something simple like black shoes, I could trust God for anything I needed.

"DEAR GOD, IT'S ME, NATHANIEL"

Elizabeth M. Thompson

A *note from Elizabeth Thompson:* "Dear God, It's Me, Nathaniel" was written from the prayers, hopes, and fears of my son in the midst of our family's greatest loss. I tried to write the prayers exactly as he prayed them. They demonstrate the innocence of a young boy's prayers as he faced the terminal illness of his beloved grandfather.

◄O►◄O►

Dear God,

It's me, Nathaniel.

Today my daddy told me that Grandpa is sick. He is not feeling too good.

Would You please heal him and help him to feel better again so we can play with our train set?

Amen.

Dear God,

It's me, Nathaniel.

My Grandpa is still sick. Daddy said Grandpa has to go see the doctor.

Would You please help my Grandpa to feel better? Please help the doctor to know what to do.

Amen.

Dear God,

It's me, Nathaniel.

Daddy told me today that Grandpa has cancer. I don't know what cancer is or why my Grandpa has it. Daddy is sad.

Would You please heal my Grandpa and help him to feel better? And would You help my Daddy to not feel sad?

Amen.

Dear God,

It's me, Nathaniel.

I saw Grandpa today. He was very tired. He didn't want to play with my trains. He didn't even want to sing songs. He just wanted to hold my hand.

Would You please heal my Grandpa so we can play together soon?

Amen.

Dear God,

It's me, Nathaniel.

Today my Grandpa went into the hospital. Why does he have to go to the hospital, God? My daddy says Grandpa may have to stay there awhile.

Would You please heal my Grandpa so he can be home?

Amen.

Dear God,

It's me, Nathaniel.

Today I went to the hospital to see my Grandpa. He looked different. His eyes were the same as always. But he looked smaller. He was quiet. I was scared. I didn't know what to do.

God, would You please heal my Grandpa?

I love him so much.

Amen.

Dear God,

It's me, Nathaniel.

Today my daddy told me that Grandpa is dying. My cat died last year, and I still miss her. I don't want my Grandpa to die.

Isn't there anything You can do to stop him from dying?

Amen.

Dear God,

It's me, Nathaniel.

My Grandpa is going home today. A nice nurse named Sarah is going to take care of him at home. I am glad he is going home. Daddy doesn't look glad, though. Today I saw him crying.

God, would You please heal my Grandpa?

We like to play with trains together.

Amen.

Dear God,

It's me, Nathaniel.

My Grandpa is still dying, Daddy told me today. We went to see Grandpa at home. He didn't play with me or talk to me. He opened his eyes, but he still didn't talk.

Would You please heal my Grandpa and help him to feel better?

Amen.

Dear God,

It's me, Nathaniel.

Today my Grandpa died.

Daddy said he is not coming back. Daddy told me that Grandpa is with You now. He told me that Grandpa is with You in heaven. He told me that in heaven, Grandpa is healed.

Grandpa is not sick anymore.

God, would You please tell Grandpa that I love him and miss him very much? Would You please tell him that we all miss him and love him?

Oh, and God, thank You for healing my Grandpa and making him feel better.

Amen.

CONSIDER THE DAFFODILS

Heidi VanderSlikke

T he daffodils on my living-room table remind me of a dear lady I knew briefly ten years ago. I can still hear her faltering voice inside my head: "A daffodil is a place to stick your nose."

It was springtime, and I was a patient in a London, Ontario, hospital. At first I had a private room because it was the only one available. Then one night I was transferred into a ward with another woman. I smiled and said hello to her as I entered the room. She mumbled something unintelligible.

Later she stretched out her arm and reached for the telephone on the nightstand. It crashed to the floor, startling both of us. I picked up the phone and placed it on her lap. She nodded awkwardly and swallowed a few times. Finally, "Thank you" came out.

Still staring at me she managed to say, "Please dial for me."

I hesitated, unsure of whom I was dealing with. Was this woman an Alzheimer's patient? Was she mentally competent? Maybe she was waiting here for a bed on the psych floor to become available. But her clear blue eyes continued to plead with me, so I punched in the numbers as she painstakingly spoke them. Thus began our friendship.

Her name was Caroline. She was in her late fifties and in the final stages of multiple sclerosis. Bill, her husband of more than thirty years, came to see her every day. In the morning he groomed her and helped her dress. After work he arrived to take her on a wheelchair tour of the hospital, feed her the evening meal, and get her ready for bed. By nine o'clock he would go home and have his own supper.

I discovered that my roommate was a beautiful person trapped inside a dying and uncooperative body. Through it all she never complained, patiently persevering as best she could. Her mind remained sharp. I learned it was worth the wait to hear what she had to say.

One morning Bill showed up with a fistful of daffodils, picked from Caroline's garden. Tears trickled down her cheeks. "A daffodil is a place to stick your nose," she said in her halting style. Her husband gently placed the flowers next to their son's graduation photo on the shelf by Caroline's bed.

I watched Caroline's gentle face as she labored to tell me the story of the daffodils. Caroline had been a teacher. After several years of marriage, she and Bill became the parents of a fine baby boy. She decided to quit teaching and stay at home with their son. When Gregory was four years old, the doctor informed Caroline that she had MS.

One autumn afternoon Caroline and Gregory planted daffodil bulbs in the flower bed. Caroline wondered if she would live to see them bloom in the spring. She watched her little boy digging enthusiastically in the dark soil and wondered how many springtimes she might see in his life. "These don't look like flowers, Mommy," said Gregory as they dropped the dry, brown bulbs into the ground.

"I know, honey," replied Caroline. "But just you wait and see how beautiful they are next spring. God will bring them to life, and they'll look just like the picture on the package."

"How does God do it, Mom? How does He bring them to life?"

"That's His business, Gregory. He creates life, and He provides for it," said Caroline, smiling at her son. "He sends the snow and the rain and the sunshine all in their seasons. Nobody knows for sure how, but somehow He breathes life into all creation, and He supplies exactly what is needed when it's needed."

Winter arrived early that year, and snow soon blanketed the yard. With the flower bed buried, Gregory and Caroline didn't talk much about spring flowers. But the boy remembered his mother's words about God's providence. The two of them would kneel beside each other every night before bedtime. He always ended his prayers with a heartfelt petition, "And please, God, take care of Mommy so she can take care of me."

Caroline added her amen and echoed his plea in her own prayers.

On a sunny April morning the following year, Gregory burst into the kitchen, eyes shining as he hid something behind his back. "I got a big surprise for you, Mom," he exclaimed. "Look what I found in the garden!"

In his chubby fingers he clutched a bouquet of golden blooms, every last daffodil from the flower bed.

"They look just like little sunshines, don't they, Mom? And look. Right here in the middle, it's the perfect place to stick your nose. God thinks of everything, doesn't He?" Gregory said with a giggle.

Caroline's eyes brightened whenever she mentioned Gregory's name. He had grown into a handsome young man, following his mom's footsteps into the teaching profession. His faith never wavered. Caroline beamed as she told me how he still prayed for her daily. Her only regret was that she might be gone before his wedding, planned for that summer. With motherly pride she said, "He was right, my little boy. God does think of everything. Even through all this sickness, He sends me everything I need, every day."

She turned her gaze toward the bouquet on the shelf. "These may be the last daffodils I see, but that's okay. I know God has better things in mind."

I went home at the end of the week, thankful to return to my family and our routine. But every year when the daffodils bloom, I think about Caroline's story and her young son's profession of faith. And I smile.

HAMSTER PRAYERS

Donita K. Paul

I 'm praying she'll have babies." The hopeful voice came from the back-seat of our car.

We hadn't even arrived home with my daughter's first pet, a teddy-bear hamster.

I smiled at Evy's wishful thinking and answered, "There has to be a daddy to have babies. We only have one hamster."

"I'll talk to God about it," answered my faithful daughter.

Cookooboo was adorable. She had soft, shaggy, apricot cream fur and tiny pink paws. Dark, perpetually wistful eyes made her look more like some enchanted fairy creature than a rodent. She lived in a birdcage with cedar chips and a glass jar she used as a den.

That night Evy prayed for all the usual things, plus one—baby hamsters, lots of baby hamsters.

"You're enjoying your Cookooboo," I said. "If she has babies, she'll have to spend time being a mommy and won't have as much time to play."

"I'll help her take care of them."

I sighed and kissed *my* baby good night.

The next night Evy sent up another petition for hamster babies.

"We only have one little cage," I reasoned. "At the rate you're praying, we'll have to take out a loan and build a hamster barn in the backyard."

Evy giggled and snuggled down under the covers.

I heard her muffled answer. "The babies will grow up, and I'll give them to the kids at school."

The next night I spotted two dollar bills on Evy's bedside table.

"Where'd you get the money?"

"Case gave it to me to buy Cookooboo an exercise ball. She needs her strength to be a good mommy."

"Your brother said that?"

"No, he said she was getting fat."

As I listened to the nightly request for babies, I had one eye open, watching the little rodent. Nah. She didn't look any rounder. Besides, there was no daddy. Cookooboo had been plucked from an aquarium at the pet store, a tank filled with little girl hamsters and cedar chips.

The next night I didn't have to chase Evy away from Cookooboo's cage and into her bed. She was already there, reading a book.

"Cookooboo nipped my finger," she complained.

I inspected the finger and thankfully saw only a tiny red mark, no broken skin.

"You'll have to be very gentle so she won't get scared," I advised as Evy got ready for her prayers.

"Yes, mommies get grumpy when they're tired."

I know where she learned that bit of wisdom. I didn't bother telling her that Cookooboo was not a mommy.

In the morning I walked into the room, opened the cage door, and scooped up the jar in which Cookooboo slept each night.

As I had every morning since that little fur ball came to our home, I dumped her out on my waking daughter.

"Time to rise and shine. Your Cookooboo wants to play."

Several somethings, pink and squirmy, remained in the jar. No hair, eyes shut, barely distinguishable as infant hamsters. Eight tiny, lima-bean babies.

Now, I'm not particularly astute that early in the morning before coffee. And no matter what time of day it is, I never like awakening to my own errors of judgment.

And it was a pretty big error. I focused on the possible, the logical, the facts. My narrow vision kept me from seeing the possibilities, the potential, the God Factor. My daughter, unhampered by years of experience, left the door open for possibilities that vary from the norm.

How often do we not pray because we already know the outcome? Or we think we do. How often are our prayers narrower than the broad blessing God would give us?

I went to college to get my education degree because I wanted to work with children. My aunt prayed I would influence millions of children. God interrupted my teaching career with a disabling illness. Now I reach many more children than I did in the classroom, because I write.

I'm still learning the valuable lesson of allowing God to be God. Even when we think we know the facts of life, it's a good idea to remember that our all-knowing Father in heaven knows more facts than we do. Even when we see the logical sequence of events, God's ways are higher and quite a bit more complicated than what we can comprehend. In the end, it's good to leave doors open for the delightful surprises God has in mind.

THE UNFAILING FAITH OF
A PRAYING CHILD

Brenda R. Coats

Mom, why are you still sick?"

I looked over at Andrew, my five-year-old son, leaning on my bedside. He stared back at me with a frustration that mirrored my own, and my heart clenched at the genuine concern in his voice. It was a somber moment, but his childish stance brought joy to my heart as he sat patiently, waiting for an answer.

As I struggled with what to tell him, I studied his face, freckled from the near-constant exposure to the summer sunlight. His mind had obviously wandered, and I chuckled silently at the sight of his squished, pudgy cheeks resting in the palms of his hands.

Snapping me back to reality, he nudged me, ready for the answer to his question. But the only reply I could offer was a shrug, accompanied by a reluctant "I don't know."

With a sigh he dropped his hands away from his face, got up from his knees, and walked away.

Poor thing, I thought as I threw the covers over my head. *He has every right to know when Mommy's going to get better.*

It had been months since I had fallen ill, and it seemed as though I had been through every medical test there was to perform. The doctors were no closer to a diagnosis, and we were left with the one thing that too often was my last resort: prayer.

One evening as I lay on my makeshift bed on the living-room sofa, I tuned my ear to the nearby dining room and listened to what had become Andrew's routine dinnertime prayer: "Dear heavenly Father, help us to have a blessing day, and help Mom to get better. In Jesus's name, amen."

The first time I heard it, I thought, *What a simple, yet heartfelt prayer.* But heartfelt or not, after months of hearing the same prayer, I found myself becoming annoyed with his repetitive, childlike appeal.

God is obviously not granting Andrew's request. When is he going to fig-ure out that God doesn't always answer our prayers the way we would like? I wondered. I was ashamed of my negative thoughts toward his innocent request to the Lord. However, I continued to wrestle, thinking, *Andrew's faith will surely be crushed if his prayer remains unanswered.*

Then I wondered, *Is it Andrew's faith that will be crushed or my own?* That question haunted me for weeks. Confronted with the painful truth that my faith was weak, I began to ask the Lord to strengthen and stretch it. Meanwhile Andrew was content to continue his plea for my healing in his predictable way.

Over the next year and a half, we were blessed with a long-awaited diagnosis and a doctor who was willing to help with a disease for which there is no known cure. Although my recovery was a slow process, I was greatly encouraged, and my faith began to flourish, not solely because of my physical progress, but because of my spiritual progress as well. I was beginning to appreciate and understand Andrew's faithfulness in prayer, even when the results were not immediate.

One afternoon, nearly two and a half years after the onset of my ill-ness, Andrew and I were on our way to pick up his sisters from school. He turned to me, tapped me on the arm, and once again asked, "Mom, why are you still sick?"

"I don't know. But do you remember when I had to rest on the couch all day and never went out of the house?"

"Uh-huh."

"Well, now I'm driving down this road to get the girls, right?"

"Right."

"And what else did we do today?"

"Um, we went to the grocery store and went out to eat."

"Yes. And what will I do when we get home?"

"I dunno." He shrugged.

"I'll make some dinner for everyone," I said, playfully pinching his knee.

He squirmed and giggled but quickly became serious.

"Yeah," he said thoughtfully. "But you still lie on the couch a lot, and you can't, you know, play ball with me and stuff like that."

"That's true," I said. "But maybe if we keep praying, I will be able to someday. What do you think?"

He responded with a dimply grin.

As we rode in silence the remainder of the way to the school, I reflected on the time when I had been bedridden. I remembered doubting that the Lord would answer Andrew's prayers and marveled at His faithfulness to me in spite of my doubts. Though I was not yet completely healed, God had truly performed a miracle in my body. But the true miracle lay in that He had taken what was once merely head knowledge of His faithfulness and transferred it deep into my heart.

PART NINE

"WOW, GOD!"

Children Thanking

Thank You that I met Alex and that we had such a great water-pistol fight. I lost, but it was fun!

—LINDSEY, age six

Help us to do a good job at school. Help everyone to get back to feeling 100 percent. Thank You for our thirty-six-inch TV and VCR and DVD surround-sound system. Thank You for everything. Help us to remember to write back tomorrow. Amen.

—PATRICK, age eleven

Thank You for not looking on the outside but on the inside. Help the weekend go smoothly. Help Sarah to be good at Gramma's. Amen.

—SEAN, age eleven

Thank You for the sun and the rain. It helps the flowers grow.

—SARAH, age seven

Comedy writer Martha Bolton shared the following incident with me:

> My sons were pretty young when I first became a staff writer
> for Bob Hope, but apparently they knew more about the comic
> legend than I thought they did. One night while my son Matt
> was saying his bedtime prayers, he said, "Thank You, God, for
> Mommy; Daddy; our dog, Chipper; my pet hamster; and thanks,
> Lord, for the memories."

Children excel in giving thanks. Gratefulness flows naturally from their sense of wonder. When my friend Jennifer had to be hospitalized with an attack of kidney stones, her son, Jordan, prayed, "Dear God, thank You that my mommy didn't die when she was taken away in the ambulance."

That's the great thing about kids. They pray for big things and little things, and both are equal in their eyes. Jordan also prayed, "Dear God, thank You that I found a rock." (I'm not sure what that did for Jennifer's self-esteem.)

Whether kids are praying about a parent's safety, a rock, or memories, they know the importance of thanking God. I want to return to the simple faith of a child who sees life as an adventure and appreciates all that is.

—Wayne

PÃO, SENHOR?

Max Lucado

from *No Wonder They Call Him the Savior*

H e couldn't have been over six years old. Dirty face, barefooted, torn T-shirt, matted hair. He wasn't too different from the other hundred thousand or so street orphans that roam Rio de Janeiro.

I was walking to get a cup of coffee at a nearby cafe when he came up behind me. With my thoughts somewhere between the task I had just finished and the class I was about to teach, I scarcely felt the tap, tap, tap on my hand. I stopped and turned. Seeing no one, I continued on my way. I'd only taken a few steps, however, when I felt another insistent tap, tap, tap. This time I stopped and looked downward. There he stood. His eyes were whiter because of his grubby cheeks and coal-black hair.

"Pão, Senhor?" ("Bread, sir?")

Living in Brazil, one has daily opportunities to buy a candy bar or sandwich for these little outcasts. It's the least one can do. I told him to come with me and we entered the sidewalk cafe. "Coffee for me and something tasty for my little friend." The boy ran to the pastry counter and made his choice. Normally, these youngsters take the food and scamper back out into the street without a word. But this little fellow surprised me.

The cafe consisted of a long bar: one end for pastries and the other for coffee. As the boy was making his choice, I went to the other end of the bar and began drinking my coffee. Just as I was getting my derailed train of thought back on track, I saw him again. He was standing in the cafe entrance, on tiptoe, bread in hand, looking in at the people. "What's he doing?" I thought.

Then he saw me and scurried in my direction. He came and stood in front of me about eye-level with my belt buckle. The little Brazilian orphan looked up at the big American missionary, smiled a smile that would have stolen your heart and said, "Obrigado." ("Thank you.") Then, nervously scratching the back of his ankle with his big toe, he added, "*Muito* obrigado." ("Thank you *very much*.")

All of a sudden, I had a crazy craving to buy him the whole restaurant.

But before I could say anything, he turned and scampered out the door.

As I write this, I'm still standing at the coffee bar, my coffee is cold, and I'm late for my class. But I still feel the sensation that I felt half an hour ago. And I'm pondering this question: If I am so moved by a street orphan who says thank you for a piece of bread, how much more is God moved when I pause to thank him—really thank him—for saving my soul?

BEDTIME RITUALS

Lori Borgman

from *Pass the Faith, Please*

I cannot think of any time better spent than cultivating an evening ritual of baths and brushing teeth followed by Mom or Dad sitting on the edge of the bed, laughing, snuggling, talking, reading from the Bible or a Bible storybook, and fielding questions like, "Where did God come from?" Bedtime rituals with small children pay dividends well into the teen years.

When our children were toddlers, we wore out every children's Bible Kenneth Taylor had a hand in creating while we tucked those kids into bed. The first favorite was *The Bible in Pictures for Little Eyes,* featuring wonderful illustrations and a brief text, followed by three or four questions. The next favorite, and you know how favorites can change from week to week, was Taylor's *Big Thoughts for Little People.* Each page featured a letter of the alphabet. "A is for Adore." "K is for Kindness." "W is for Worship." Each page was richly illustrated and included text that explained the big idea and several questions that required careful observation of the marvelously detailed illustrations. All of those books still sit on our shelves today.

We also used the bedtime rituals to teach our children the mechanics of prayer. We told them that prayer is simply talking to God. Pray simple prayers with your children, encourage them to pray, and teach them to pray. And don't rush. The dishes will wait, voice mail can catch the phone, and odds are there's absolutely nothing on television worth watching. Don't rush. Of course, that's much easier said than done.

I remember the prayer of the small child who listed everything she was thankful for when she prayed before bedtime. She gave thanks for her Big Wheel and her teacher and the sheep on her wallpaper border and her pillow and her family and her family's family and for food and for the birds.

…and I was thinking, *Let's wrap this up soon; I have some things to do.*

And she was thankful for the rabbits and that she found the missing piece to Candy Land and for her toothbrush and for Linda, who sings praise songs in the car when she drives kids places.

…and I was thinking, *If she keeps this up, we're going to have to put a rug in here; this hardwood floor is killing my knees.*

And she was thankful for the rain and the sun and that the police officer with the radar gun didn't catch Mommy speeding and for Jesus and God and the Holy Spirit and, oh yes! she loves them the same and doesn't have favorites.

…and I was wishing this would come to an end soon when I was struck with the realization that I was wishing an end to a prayer of thanksgiving and praise to the God of the universe. Here was a child building a faith that would carry her through who knows what in the future, and I was willing to cut it short in order to get to my very important list of things to do.

I determined that I would never rush a kid again. Still, at times I'd get antsy during these rituals. Did they never tire of the same songs, the same prayers over and over? Not after a hundred times or a thousand times? No, never. And yet those five, ten, or fifteen minutes strengthened our relationship and planted the seeds of their relationships with God. Those few minutes often had a way of putting an entire day into perspective. We spend so much time living and planning for the next half hour, the next week, and the next holiday that the time we have today can slip away right under our noses.

DISABLED DREAMS

Tamara Boggs

from *Children Are a Blessing from the Lord*

> All your [children] will be taught by the LORD,
> and great will be your children's peace.
> —ISAIAH 54:13

> "For I know the plans I have for you," declares the
> LORD, "plans to prosper you and not to harm you,
> plans to give you hope and a future."
> —JEREMIAH 29:11

S o, what can we expect for Christiana's future?" Don's words were casual, but his voice held an underlying tension.

The social worker at the children's hospital hesitated, then said, "Well, she can certainly train for a vocational job in high school and most likely be competitive in a vocational setting. She possibly could live independently or in a group home setting, and she even might be able to marry. You just never know." She spoke as if she were telling us good news about our seven-year-old mildly autistic and mentally handicapped daughter.

Don and I sat in silence. It had been a long day of IQ testing, language and speech testing, sensory integration dysfunction testing, and interviews for Don and me. I had come to the hospital hoping to gain some further understanding of our middle child that would help me parent her better. She was "a study" as my Grandma Stannie would say.

I had never thought about her long-term future. Although the room was plenty warm, I shivered. *Might be able to many? Possibly live independently?* These were things I had taken for granted for all my children. Not that they all needed to marry or go to college or leave home the day after their eighteenth birthdays, but, without thinking about it, I had expected that they all could do these things if they chose to do them. I had certain dreams for them. I hoped they would experience the same joy, growth, and sense of accomplishment I had experienced in life.

Christiana bounded into the room ahead of the speech pathologist who had been entertaining her during our debriefing. Christiana threw herself onto the couch next to me and hugged me. She had enjoyed all of the attention. It wasn't often that she got to be with both Don and me without her brother and sister.

I smiled down into her face, radiant with affection. I fought back the tears threatening to fill my eyes. *She doesn't know what she might miss. Oh, Christiana, my sweet Christiana.* I pushed her page-boy bangs off her forehead and kissed her.

The director stood and offered her hand. "If you have any more questions, don't hesitate to call."

I shook her hand. "Thank you for all you've done."

"Yes," said Don. "This has been very helpful."

Christiana's arms were wrapped around my waist. "Are we going home now? Can I have a treat for being good?"

"Yes. You've been very patient, Christiana," I said.

Cookie in hand, Christiana crawled into the van, and we headed home. I thought she would be exhausted. We had gotten up earlier than usual to make the hour drive to the hospital that morning. But Christiana was in a silly mood, singing and talking.

Don hadn't said much since we left the office. I could tell he was disturbed. "Is something the matter?" I asked. My extroverted need to "talk things out" made me think he might need to talk.

He shook his head and glanced back at Christiana. "Later," he said. Tears filled his eyes, and he squeezed my hand.

I quickly looked out at the road.

Christiana began to talk to several pretend test-takers, herself in the role of the test administrator. Playacting was a common way she processed whatever had happened during her day.

"Okay, now we will have lunch," Christiana said to her patients. "You may have anything you want. Pizza and ice cream? Okay. Who wants to pray? Ashley? Okay.

"Dear God, thank you for us to take tests today and thank you for the love and thank you for Jesus Christ to come and be born in a stable. Amen. That was very good.…"

I stopped listening. Christiana's prayer repeated in my thoughts. *Thank you for the tests…for the love…for Jesus. Thank you, thank you, thank you.* I smiled. What was the value of jobs or even independent living or marriage in light of the realities of God's love and Jesus Christ "born in a stable."

As I let the simple faith expressed by Christiana's prayer fill me, I felt God prying her loose from my fear-filled grasp. She was not my child to control. She was God's child. She did not need to fulfill my dreams for her. God had a plan and a purpose for her life, a first-rate plan that we would discover together.

The Day the Sandman Came

Gigi Graham

from *Weatherproof Your Heart*

> You know that the testing of your faith develops
> perseverance. Perseverance must finish its work
> so that you may be mature and complete,
> not lacking anything.
>
> —JAMES 1:3-4

The afternoon thunderstorm had rolled on and the sun was out once again. Soon the children would crawl out from various corners of the house like so many little bugs after dark. Summer was only half over, and I had six more weeks to try to find creative ways to entertain six energetic children.

Suddenly I spotted the old sandbox.

"Let's fix it up!" I announced.

After gathering the troops, we pulled weeds and cleaned up the area. Then we were off to the local sand company. We had been told that our sandbox would require about five tons of sand. Not really knowing how much five tons would be, we took the van, loaded with buckets and old garbage cans.

With our containers filled, we returned home. Our son backed the van around, leaving a few tire tracks in the wet grass. He dumped the sand

and drove back across the grass, this time breaking off a small tree limb in the process and receiving a sharp tongue-lashing from me.

When we looked at the sandbox, we saw that the sand filled only one small corner! A quick call to the company confirmed that, for a small fee, they would deliver the remaining sand that very afternoon. I cautioned them to send their lightest truck and their best driver, as the yard was wet from recent heavy rains.

When the truck arrived, I showed the driver where the sandbox was located and, as he began to back around the house, I followed. To my dismay, the truck loaded with sand was making deep trenches in the soft ground. Maneuvering the rear of the truck into position, he took several large branches from overhanging trees. Oh, well! Maybe the children's enjoyment of their sandbox would be worth all the trouble!

Then it happened. The driver got stuck in the wet earth. The more he accelerated, the deeper he sank, until his big truck began to slide down the hill toward the lake, plowing a gaping hole on its way. By now, he was in up to his axles, and I suggested we call the sand company and ask for help.

An hour later, a large tow truck arrived. The driver backed around, leaving more black trenches, and put a cable around truck number one. The more he tugged and pulled, the larger the hole grew. Then he, too, got stuck, digging into the yard, breaking sprinkler pipes, splintering branches, and uprooting small trees. Another call to the company resulted in truck number three, the cab of an eighteen-wheeler!

About eight o'clock that evening, after five-and-a-half hours of mass destruction, all three trucks pulled out of our yard. When we assessed the damage, there was the gaping hole, the broken sprinkler pipes sticking up like so many broken bones, ugly black tracks across our lawn, ripped trees, and five tons of sand—not in, but *beside* the sandbox. And a bill for the sand and two tow trucks!

Much later, as I was tucking the eight-year-old in bed, he prayed: "And thank You, Lord, for the exciting day and for all the entertainment we had!"

In spite of everything, I had to chuckle. I hadn't thought about the day's disasters in terms of "entertainment." Nor had I thought about thanking God for all the excitement. Yet falling asleep with thanksgiving on your tongue—no matter what the circumstances—was certainly an improvement over what had been on *my* tongue and heart that evening.

No wonder the Scripture entreats us to be more like children!

Just Say "Wow!"

Barbara Eubanks

As adults, we get in a rut with our pious way of praying, and we often have an exaggerated opinion of our ability to impress God. We sound as though we are speaking in stained-glass tones and mistakenly think that we can influence God with our high-sounding monologues. Often it takes a child to awaken some of us to a genuine way of communicating with God, a novel way to praise Him in our prayers. From my granddaughter Bethany, I learned a new way to do just that.

Bethany was spending a few days with my husband and me. As usual we tried to find activities that would make her visit a memorable one. We rode the horse, went swimming, had some children over for her to play with, ate at McDonald's, and did the many things grandparents do to entertain a grandchild. When bedtime came, I was totally exhausted; she was still spry as a chipmunk.

I finally called bedtime and went upstairs to tuck her in. I asked if she would like for us to have our prayer time together. She answered, "Sure."

I was expecting a typical child's prayer such as "Now I lay me down to sleep…"

Her response not only surprised me but also taught me a lesson in prayer. "Gram, let's just do 'wow' prayers tonight." I told her I wasn't quite sure what a "wow" prayer was. She told me, "You just name the good things God has done and the good things that happened that day, and then say, 'Wow, God!'"

She then began to name the fun-filled activities of the day. After each one, she said, "Wow, God!" Then she named the people who are special in her life and thanked God for them in her own special way. Once more after each one she named, she said, "Wow, God!"

From Bethany I learned a fresh way to genuinely praise God in my daily prayers. I learned to name the people for whom I am thankful. For the beauty of this world; for His ever-abiding presence; for continued mercy, grace, and forgiveness; and for giving us His Son, I now say "Wow, God! You teach me new things daily, sometimes through unexpected sources."

> Then a voice came from the throne, saying, "Praise our God, all
> you His servants and those who fear Him, both small and great!"
> (Revelation 19:5, NKJV)

A HOLY PRESENCE

Lois Pecce

S ometimes it takes the simple expressions of a child's heart to remind us of what prayer really is: opening our hearts to God as to a friend. Prayers at our house, especially at mealtime, can become hurried and banal.

Our neighbor's five-year-old daughter refreshed my perspective one day with her sweet, impassioned plea.

Chelsea frequently came to play with our granddaughter. One afternoon we invited her to have lunch with us, and she offered to say the blessing.

"Dear Jesus, I wish that You could come down and eat with us." She paused and sighed. "But I know that You're too busy, and You have to stay up there in heaven. I really wish You weren't so busy. Amen."

"Thank you, Chelsea. That was a beautiful prayer."

Her plaintive desire for the presence of Jesus reminded me that of all the things we might ask for, the one thing Christ never denies us is His Presence.

"Do you know, Chelsea, Jesus *does* come when you invite Him?"

"He does? How?"

"You can't see Him with your eyes, just like you can't see the angels. But the Bible tells us Jesus promised that wherever people come together in His name—to pray to Him—He will be there with them. Do you understand what I said?"

She nodded slowly, sorting it out in her mind.

"I'm going to tell you something else that I want you to always remember," I said, placing my hand on her shoulder to focus her attention. "Jesus and God are *never* too busy for you. They love you very much, Chelsea, and They will never be too busy to hear you or to be near you."

She looked into my eyes. "Really?"

"Really."

Indeed, I felt the Lord's holy presence fill the room as her face lit with joy. He had come down by His Spirit to answer the call of her heart and the silent prayer of mine as I'd searched for words to reassure her.

Why, I wondered, *had I not sought this blessed Presence at every meal? Why had I been content so often to utter hurried words with thoughts more of other things than of our unseen Guest?*

━◦━◦━

Almost two years later, during a school break, Chelsea was playing at our house when she learned that we planned to have her favorite vegetable for lunch. I invited her to stay.

"Do you still pray before you eat?" she asked.

"Yes. Would you like to pray for us?"

She nodded happily. "Dear God and Jesus, thank You that You always come down to be with us when we eat."

She remembered!

PART TEN

"IN THE NAME OF JESUS"

Children Healing

Dear God, please help my brother Austin's brain that is broken. He needs You to fix it so he can talk better.

    —JACOB, age three, praying for his autistic brother

Thank You for healing me when I was sick. Thanks for healing me when I stepped on a tack.

    —BETH, age seven

Help the shooter at the school in San Diego. Help the families that the two kids came from that got killed. Help everyone that was hurt and wounded. Help it not to happen again. In Jesus's name, amen.

    —SCOTT, age nine

Dear God, why is it that people keep breaking bones? Why can't bones be made of steel?

    —JORDAN, age nine

C hildren should be encouraged to pray for healing. Their faith is simple and pure. They have a direct line with the Father, and they ask without qualifying their petitions.

We need to pay attention. Too often we allow our doubts to seep into our prayers. Not kids.

Jesus encouraged us to develop kid-faith. When He asked the Father to raise Lazarus from the dead, He demonstrated what that looks like. His prayer was simple.

"Father, I thank you that you have heard me. I knew that you always hear me, but I said this for the benefit of the people standing here, that they may believe that you sent me" (John 11:41-42).

With that short prayer, Jesus called Lazarus back to life by commanding him to come out. Jesus didn't ask God for anything. He thanked His Father for hearing Him. He added that He didn't need to thank His Father but that He did it for those who were present, to strengthen their faith. This childlike trust goes beyond asking. Jesus knew that the answer was already on the way.

To develop kid-faith, we must follow the lead of children and know that God sends the answers even as we make our requests known.

—*Wayne*

THE LAYING ON OF HANDS

Richard J. Foster

from *Prayer*

T he laying on of hands in itself does not heal the sick—it is Christ who heals the sick. The laying on of hands is a simple act of obedience that quickens our faith and gives God the opportunity to impart healing. Often people will add the accompanying means of anointing with oil, following the counsel of James 5:14. Like many others I have discovered that, when praying for people with the laying on of hands, I sometimes detect a gentle flow of energy. I have found that I cannot make the flow of heavenly life happen, but I can stop it. If I resist or refuse to be an open conduit for God's power to come into a person, it will stop. Also, a spirit of hate or resentment arrests the flow of life immediately. Unforgiveness on the part of the person receiving ministry is also a roadblock.

Obviously, common sense and a respect for the integrity of others will keep us from engaging in this work lightly or carelessly. We simply do not go around plopping our hands on anyone we please. Paul cautions about laying hands on people indiscriminately because it might bring them into things for which they are not ready (1 Tim. 5:22). Sanctified common sense will teach us what is appropriate at any given time.

I might add that while we adults struggle with this idea of the laying on of hands, children have no difficulty with it. I was once called to a home to pray for a seriously ill baby. Her four-year-old brother was in the room, and so I told him I needed his help in praying for his baby sister.

He was delighted to help, and I was delighted to have him, for I know that children can often pray with unusual effectiveness. He climbed up into the chair beside me. "Let's play a little game," I suggested. "Since we know that Jesus is always with us, let's suppose that he is sitting over in that chair across from us. He is waiting patiently for us to focus our attention on him. When we see him and the love in his eyes, we start thinking more about his love than about how sick Julie is. He smiles, gets up, and comes over to us. When that happens, we both put our hands on Julie, and as we do, Jesus puts his hands right on top of ours. He releases his healing light right into your little sister sort of like a whole bunch of soldiers who go in and fight the bad germs until they are all gone. Okay?" Seriously the boy nodded. Together we prayed just as I had described it to him, and then we thanked God that this was the way it was going to be. Amen. While we prayed, I sensed that my small prayer partner had exercised unusual faith.

The next morning Julie was perfectly well. Now, I cannot prove to you that our little prayer game made Julie well. All I know is that Julie was healed, and that was all I needed to know.

"It's Okay, Mommy"

Michelle Medlock Adams

A s I watered my fern on our front porch, I studied the yard. We had just moved in two weeks before, and the former owners had neglected the yard for what appeared to be years.

There's so much work to do, I thought.

Our yard looked like a jungle, but not a lush, green, thriving jungle. No, our yard looked more like a jungle that had been through some sort of freak chemical spill, killing all of the grass and leaving only hideous weeds.

But we were determined. The whole family decided to pitch in. Jeff began trimming the overgrown hedges, and the girls and I started picking up debris and large sticks from the yard. After an hour or so, I retreated to the cool air conditioning for a Diet Coke break. Moments later, Allyson, then four years old, came tearing into the house, screaming.

"It bit me! It bit me!" she hollered, holding the calf of her right leg.

"What bit you?" I asked, expecting to see a mosquito bite.

"I don't know, but it hurt!"

I knelt down and inspected Ally's calf. There was a red, raised bump, but nothing too terrible looking.

"I think you're going to live," I teased. "It was probably just a fire ant or a pesky mosquito."

As any mom would do, I put bug-bite ointment on the red bump and kissed Ally on the head.

"That should make it feel better," I said.

Allyson wiped her tears on the bottom of her untucked shirt and decided to take a soda break too. The crying had stopped, and everything seemed all right. We worked out in the yard until dusk before calling it a day.

As I gave Allyson her bath that night, I noticed the red bump had become larger, but it didn't look alarming. So I slathered more ointment on it and put her to bed. Daddy prayed with her and Abby, and we all retreated to our rooms for a good night's rest.

The next morning I was awakened by the sunlight spilling in through our bedroom blinds.

It's going to be a beautiful day, I thought.

Then my eyes glanced at the alarm clock. Seven thirty-five.

"Seven thirty-five! Oh no! Jeff, we overslept!"

I had twenty-five minutes to get the girls and myself ready, pack lunches, and drive them to school and me to work. It would take a miracle.

The morning was a blur. The girls dressed and fed themselves while I threw on a pantsuit, brushed my teeth, put my hair in a clip, and packed their lunches. On the way out the door, I put their hair in ponytails, and we piled into our Ford Explorer.

I dropped them off at school, drove as if I were in the Indy 500, and rushed inside my office at 8:32, only two minutes late.

Just as I plopped down into my office chair, the phone rang.

Oh no, I thought. *My boss must've noticed I came in a little late.*

"Mrs. Adams, I am calling about Allyson," I heard the voice say on the other end of the line. "Have you looked at her leg? She has a very serious bite of some sort, and I think you need to get her to a doctor."

I bit my lip, realizing that in all of the confusion that morning, I hadn't even looked at her leg.

"We were working in the yard yesterday, and she told us that something had bitten her, but we didn't know what," I said.

"It looks a lot like a wound from a brown recluse spider. I don't say that to scare you, but I think you need to get her to the doctor right away."

I could feel hot tears welling in my eyes. I couldn't believe what I was hearing. We had just moved to Texas, so I wasn't up on all of the poisonous insects in the area, but I had heard of the brown recluse spider, and I knew it could be bad.

"I'll be right there," I said, hanging up.

Minutes later I was at Ally's school, inspecting her leg. The bite was no longer red; it had turned dark, almost black, surrounded by a perfect circle of purplish-red. It was so swollen that the bump was visible beneath her pant leg.

I called a nearby pediatrician from my cell phone, described Allyson's wound, and told the nurse that we were on our way. Then I called Jeff and my mother and blubbered a few minutes to each of them. All the while, Allyson sat quietly in the backseat. She was very calm.

That's probably the effect of the poison in her system, I reasoned. She is probably going into some sort of shock.

I sobbed even louder.

A sweet little voice from the backseat whispered, "It's okay, Mommy. I already prayed about my leg."

Amazed, I studied her through my rearview mirror.

Allyson had peace because she had already given the situation to the Father. At age four, she knew the most important thing to do in a crisis: pray. At twenty-nine years of age, I had totally forgotten to pray.

Allyson remained calm throughout the hysterical outbursts of her mother, the poking and prodding of the doctor and nurses, the injection of medicine into her leg—all of it. She was a pillar of strength, and I was a bowl of Jell-O.

I finally calmed down once I heard the doctor say, "She is going to be just fine. If she were going to take a turn for the worse, it would have happened already. Just watch the wound overnight and bring her back tomorrow for another shot."

I nodded, thanked the doctor, and hugged Allyson so hard she said, "Ouch."

Allyson's leg took a few weeks to heal, but eventually all signs of the bite disappeared. Memories of that spider bite, however, will stick with me forever. It taught me a very important lesson: Go to God first.

Even though I prayed over my children every day, I didn't think to run to God when the spider-bite scare arose. I tried to handle it myself, and when it seemed too big, I became overwhelmed with emotion.

As ashamed as I was about my lack of instinctive prayer, I was equally proud of Allyson's automatic prayer response. I had taught her well; I just needed a refresher course.

ONE CHILD'S PRAYER

Patricia Stebelton

I heaved a sigh. It was that time again. "Come on kids! Turn off the TV and hurry up! It's time for devotions."

My voice held more enthusiasm than I felt as I herded them toward the family room where their dad waited with the family Bible.

My secret prayer was that one magic night our family devotions would cease to be a time of challenge and child discipline and become the spiritual experience I longed for. The reality that this was not that magic night struck with force during Bible-reading time. It began with separating eight-year-old Michael from five-year-old Mark and ended with warning our daughter, Kelly, about further interruptions.

In truth, I was having trouble keeping my own head into devotions. My restless thoughts kept wandering back to the disturbing story I'd heard in town earlier that afternoon.

◄○►◄○►

From the time I parked the car and walked up the street, I heard people whispering. I caught mere pieces of conversation wherever I went.

"It's such a tragedy! Imagine it happening to the same family twice."

"I know. It's as if they were cursed."

"They say the mother acts so strange."

By the time I reached the beauty shop, I was filled with curiosity. Climbing into the chair, I couldn't wait to ask, "What's the whole town buzzing about?"

My stylist was astonished. "Didn't you hear about that bad car crash last Friday?"

"What crash?"

She rushed into the story with relish. "The Lewis girls were driving home from high school on that back road by the cemetery, with the oldest at the wheel. Her sister was riding in the backseat with a girlfriend. They must have all been talking or something—no one knows for sure. Best guess is that the girls never saw the train coming when they crossed the railroad tracks."

"*A train?*" I exclaimed, horrified. "Were they all—?"

My stylist shook her head, moving to the back of my head. "Not all of them. The older sister, who was driving, lived, but she's really not herself. She refuses to believe that any of it happened. I guess she can't deal with it yet. It's such a shame. The family now has only one child left out of three."

I was confused. "I know there were two killed in the crash, but I thought you said the other girl in the backseat was a friend."

"That's right, but the family had an older son."

"*Had* a son?"

"Last year he was shot and killed late one night by a nervous farmer."

"How bizarre! How sad! That poor family!" I exclaimed softly.

"Exactly."

"Do the parents have a strong faith?" I was hopeful.

"Oh, no one dares talk to the mother about God!" she whispered, confidentially, brushing my neck. "They say she yells and practically flies at anyone who mentions God, including her priest."

"That's too bad," I murmured. "They've been through a lot. Knowing God would help!"

◄○►◄○►

They've been through a lot! still echoed in my head. The family room was still. My husband had finished reading the Bible. All eyes were focused on me, waiting.

"*Mom!*" Kelly said, nudging me. "It's prayer time."

I looked into each of my children's faces wondering how I'd feel if I lost them. I drew in a deep breath and said, "Before prayers, I have a story to tell you about a poor family in town who no longer has two of their children, and they are very, very sad."

After the story when each of us took a turn to pray, little Mark, with the gravest of expressions, prayed, "Dear God, please help the sad family who lost their children. Amen."

I wiped at a tear from my eye and finished our prayer time. Later that night I wrote Mark's prayer in a hasty note, adding a short explanation about our prayer time, and sent it on to Mrs. Lewis. *Small comfort at a safe distance,* I thought, guiltily, feeling inadequate to do more.

In the next six months, God taught me some important faith lessons, and I was excited about what He might teach me next, until one morning when a scary idea started dogging my thoughts, *Stop by and talk to Mrs. Lewis about the Lord today.*

I pushed that thought away. Surely God wouldn't ask me to do that. Didn't He remember how Mrs. Lewis reportedly reacted to people who talked about God?

Not only did the thought persist, but a new sense of urgency now accompanied it. I definitely was not comfortable with the idea of visiting Mrs. Lewis. It gave me a strange feeling in the pit of my stomach that I refused to put a name to. I made excuses. My day was planned. There wasn't time for anything else. I jammed my mind full of demanding errands and started for town, forgetting that I had to pass the Lewis's home.

Two houses before the Lewis home, that nagging thought came back to me with the force of a hurricane, and I found myself turning into their drive. Switching off the engine, I sat petrified. *There is no way I can get out of this van and up to that door.* Fear was what I had been refusing to face. I faced it now, wanting to leave immediately, but somehow my shaking legs carried me all the way to the back door. Raising a timid hand, I pushed the bell.

Please let her not be home, I prayed. A long, lonely minute passed. I rang it again, then hurriedly turned as I contemplated running to my van. Hearing a noise behind me, I swallowed hard and turned to face an open door. A slender woman of medium height stood staring at me.

"Yes?" she asked.

With a dry mouth I stammered, "G-good morn-n-ing. Uh, we've never met…but my name is—"

Mrs. Lewis interrupted me. "What did you say your name was?"

I repeated my name.

"Didn't you send me a note a few months ago?"

"Yes," I answered slowly.

"Your little boy prayed for us?"

"Yes, he did." Gathering more confidence, I gave her a weak smile.

"Please come in," she said.

I swallowed once more. "I'd love to."

This was not the wild-eyed, irrational, fire-breathing woman I expected to find. Her home was cool and tastefully furnished, but while the sun was shining brightly outside, all the shades were drawn and the rooms dark as if they, too, grieved with the family.

Mrs. Lewis walked me around her large living room and showed me pictures of all her children—the two who were gone and the one who remained. I listened as she talked about each of them. Somehow the conversation gradually turned to the subject of God. I shared with her how God understands her pain because He, too, lost a Son. His peace and love are gifts waiting to be received. In the quietness of her living room, this wounded, hurting mother invited the Jesus of healing into her heart to be her personal Savior that morning.

What a joy! I was jubilant when I said good-bye to Mrs. Lewis that amazing day she met the Savior, and I was so excited that I could hardly wait to share with my family—especially Mark—what God had done with his prayer. God had used it not only to gently open the door of the house but to prepare the heart door of this grieving lady. When I made a return visit at a later time, I found her with a peaceful heart, living in a sunlit house where Jesus now lived too.

Were our nightly devotional times any less chaotic in the days to come? No. But I looked at them in a new light, no longer discounting this time together as ineffective or unproductive. God showed me that He can work in any situation to touch hearts in unusual ways. My job is to remain faithful and available and to listen carefully to the prayers of the very young.

SIMPLE FAITH

Lisa Eblen Wiener

Two-year-old Allison's brown eyes narrowed with concern.

"What's wrong with your leg, Mommy?" she asked one morning. She had noticed me limping down the hallway from my bedroom into the living room.

"Oh, it's nothing. I probably just lay on it wrong." My right leg felt stiff and sore, as if I had been sleeping on it in an awkward position. It hurt to walk on it, but I figured the problem would work itself out in a day or two.

I turned to go into the kitchen to prepare breakfast, but before I could take another step, Allison surprised me by wrapping her arms completely around my leg, nearly causing me to fall. I couldn't move. I felt the added warmth from her body atop the warmth from my robe. Before I could ask what she was doing, she began to pray.

"Esus," she said. Then she mumbled something I couldn't understand and finished with, "Please make Mommy's leg all better. In Esus's name, amen!"

Just as suddenly as she had grabbed my leg, she let go. The entire episode lasted but a few seconds. I felt free from my "bondage" but stunned by what she'd just done. As I walked away, I realized that my leg was fine. There was absolutely no pain in it anymore.

"Does it feel better, Mommy?" Allison asked, her large eyes round with hope. I walked around the room a bit more, making sure to put my usual weight on my right leg. To my amazement, I still felt no pain.

"Yes." I replied. "Allison, I think God just healed Mommy's leg."

I knelt to give her a hug. Placing my hands on her shoulders, I looked into her eyes. "Thank you for praying for me." As we embraced, I marveled at the faith of one so small, so young. Her soft, brown curls brushed my cheek as she skipped away, returning to her world of dolls, stuffed animals, and make-believe.

"Good!" she said over her shoulder, as if her work was done. My eyes moistened. I hadn't even thought to pray about my leg, but for Allison it was a natural response. Mommy hurt; God could help. It was as simple as that.

A PRAYER OF FAITH

Diana J. Baker

P lease, Mommy, please," my daughter Shannon begged. "Can't we go outside now?"

"In a few minutes," I answered. "I have to finish the dishes first."

"But, Mommy," Shannon said, "you can see us out the window."

It was a beautiful, sunny day, and I remembered how much I had enjoyed being outdoors when I was young. Although I really wasn't sure about allowing my sometimes bossy three-year-old to watch my two-year-old, it was hard to resist Shannon's pleading eyes. The seminary campus was safe, and I knew my neighbors well. I could even see a friend a few doors down enjoying outdoor activities with her children. Maybe it would be okay to let my girls go out as long as they stayed where I could see them from my kitchen window.

"All right," I said to Shannon, "you can go out. But you have to stay where I can see you from the window. I'll come too when I finish the dishes."

I put the girls' shoes on, checked on baby Stevie in the playpen, and helped Jenny down the steps of our mobile home. I showed Shannon where they were to play and returned to the kitchen.

As I stood at the sink washing dishes, I thanked God for the peace and security of the seminary campus and for the great church He had led us to. I marveled at the things Shannon was learning in Sunday school. She seemed very excited about her class and her new teacher. She had even begun quoting Bible verses.

The move to the seminary had not been an easy one. Leaving the security of Larry's accounting job, selling our four-bedroom home, and moving with two small children and a baby on the way had been quite a challenge. However, God had provided for us in an awesome way in the seven months we had been at the seminary.

Suddenly loud crying in the yard caught my attention. I looked out the window and saw Jenny lying on the ground. Before I could make a move to help her, Shannon ran to her, laid her hands on top of Jenny's head, and prayed loudly, "In the name of Jesus, be healed!" Immediately after the prayer, Shannon ran back to the toys she had been playing with, leaving Jenny lying on the ground crying.

I couldn't help but laugh as I dried my hands and hurried out the door. Evidently, Shannon thought she had done her duty by praying for Jenny. She obviously expected Jesus to take over and care for Jenny from that point on.

I reached Jenny, helped her up, checked for scratches, and gave her a reassuring hug. She was fine and wasted little time getting back to her toys.

"Thank you for praying for Jenny," I said to Shannon. "But the next time, try putting a little action with your prayers. At least help your sister up if she falls again."

"Okay, Mommy," Shannon replied as she impulsively ran over and planted a kiss on her sister's forehead.

My heart's desire is to have the kind of childlike faith Shannon demonstrated that day. Prayer was her initial response to a painful situation, and her prayer was bold and to the point. She knew Jesus had the power to heal, and she fully expected her sister to be healed when she prayed for her in Jesus's name. I want my relationship with God and my faith in Him to increase my expectation level so that I can pray for others with the same boldness and confidence Shannon exhibited in her prayer for Jenny.

A Brother's Gift

Emily Sue Harvey

W ho wants to pray first?" I asked my three children. They lounged before the parsonage's open fireplace, embedded in deep-pile, autumn gold carpet, while I occupied the fireside easy chair.

"I do!" Seven-year-old David's hand shot up. He was the enthusiastic, adventuresome Harvey sibling, upon whom two older sisters doted—especially eleven-year-old Angie, his proverbial little mother hen. Pam, at thirteen, already inhabited another planet most of the time.

"Great, David," I said, trying to repress a grin as firelight strobed over his freckled, Howdy Doody–happy features.

While Lee, my pastor-husband, did church visitation, I gathered the children nightly for relaxed devotions. Our answered prayers had run from interesting to awesome. Before David led in prayer, Angie shared one such result.

"You remember Joanne, the girl in my class?" she asked, eyes glimmering with excitement.

"The one who's really poor, and nobody plays with her?" David asked.

"Uh-huh." Angie smiled at him. "We prayed for her. Remember, Mama, you told me to be her friend and play with her at recess? I did what you told me. And she's so sweet! I just love her. And y'know, other kids started playing with her too. She's started laughing and talking; she was too shy before. She acts so happy now."

"That's wonderful, Angie," I said softly.

David squirmed and wiggled up on his knees, clasped his hands before him, and began to pray: "Lord, thank You for helping Joanne not be shy anymore. Thanks for making her happy now and helping her get friends. It's real sad when you got no playmates. Bless Daddy while he visits sick people. Make 'em well, Lord. Bless Daddy, Mama, Angie, and Pam, too. Thank You for Mama and Daddy. And thank You for Jesus. In Jesus's name, amen."

When devotions ended, he scuttled off to bed, and I thought, *How simple and powerful his faith.*

◄○►◄○►

Within weeks of David's childlike prayer, a sudden, tragic accident took Angie's life. What unimaginable anguish. *Dear Lord, she'd been my shadow, myself at times, my soul-child.* I felt gutted. How could we get through life without our little nursemaid? Another great concern was *How will David cope?* After all, he and his sister had been unusually close, spending most of their free time together.

Amid the devastation I was concerned that David didn't seem to grasp the enormity of what had happened to his protective, playmate-sister. While teenage Pam grieved with her father and me, David seemed detached from it all, going about his play with new intensity. I wanted him in our tight little circle of grief, and when days passed and his busyness persisted, I began to feel my anger rising over his seeming indifference to the family's sorrow.

For weeks Pam, Lee, and I grieved. Sometimes we gathered in Angie's room, lounging on her bed in silence or reminiscing about happy things. David remained preoccupied, constantly leaving the house.

One day I saw him laboring across the backyard, dirty as a little street urchin. "What in the world are you doing with that shovel and bucket?" I called to him as he disappeared over the hill and out of sight.

"Just wait and see," came his reply. "It's a surprise."

No doubt, he's off on another of his fantasy escapades. Soon, visiting pals joined the clandestine fun. As the days passed, my disappointment piqued. Yet David continued disappearing over that blasted hill with an irritating gleam in his eye. He rarely mentioned Angie.

Will he forget her? I agonized. Several times I started to talk to him about it, but something always stopped me.

I was still grieving so much that I delayed resuming our evening devotions. Dealing with Angie's empty space would have been too painful.

Each night before bedtime, David still knelt beside his bed and said his simple, trusting prayers, ones I barely heard as I passed his door. *At least he is still in touch with God,* I thought, *even if he is removed from our grim drama.*

I didn't expect him to grieve as I did, but he could at least have mentioned his sister's name or shown some emotion. His loss was great, so why didn't he speak of it?

One day, weeks later, David dashed into the house, all grimy and sweaty, grabbed my hand, and tugged me outside to the knoll of the hill. "Close your eyes," he said, then carefully guided me over and down the slope and halted at the site. "Now you can look," he said, his voice dancing with exuberance.

I opened my eyes and gasped. David had made a miniature pond—not the kind an adult would make, but it was beautiful. A small bridge of stacked, split logs provided a crude ramp big enough for me to walk right out to the center of the water.

"I made it for Angie."

From atop a tall pole on the shallow shore flapped a white banner. Meticulously printed in David's neat handwriting, it read ANGIE SHILOH POND.

I was so overcome I couldn't speak. *And I thought he didn't understand.*

"What do you think about it?" He gazed expectantly at me.

How had I not *known?* The gleam in his eyes that I had resented was determination and purpose. I felt like sinking into the marsh.

"Angie would be so proud that you built this in her honor." *So very proud.*

That night when David knelt beside his bed to pray, I quietly joined him. I sat on his bed as he prayed, "Dear Lord, I miss Angie a lot. Especially at recess time 'cause she always walked over and spoke to me and sometimes even hugged me. But Mama and Daddy said she's with You now. So I guess I'm happy. I don't always feel happy. My stomach hurts a lot when I think about Angie being gone. When it does, I don't feel so good. Please make me better, Lord. Bless Mama and Daddy and Pam. In Jesus's name, amen."

Why hadn't I taken time to listen? I swiped my wet cheeks as he sat on the side of his bed and tugged off his sock. I noticed the grubby, callused little hands.

"You know why I built that pond, don't you, Mama?"

"Tell me, honey."

"I prayed and told God I wanted to do something for Angie. I just had to do something, y'know—*big.*" Blue eyes turned up toward my face. I saw the sorrow in their depths. And the dark shadows beneath them.

"She didn't have much of a life, did she?" he asked.

"Why do you say that?"

He tugged off the other sock. "Eleven years isn't long to live, is it? That's why I couldn't do a dime thing. I had to do a—a *dollar thing.*" He grew still for a long moment, reflecting solemnly on that. "I think she knows."

I nodded, too choked to speak.

For months I allowed the banner and the rough-hewn bridge to remain on the back corner of our lot. I couldn't bring myself to part with it. Rain faded the letters and the wood began to crumble, but the message remained alive. Time did not diminish its comfort.

Late one afternoon I stood on the ramp in silence. And then birdsong penetrated my haze, sweetly transporting me to a place of peace.

I knew what David, with a child's simplicity, already knew: In the Lord we never truly lose someone we love. *Thank you, David, my son.*

I blew a kiss and whispered, "I love you, Angie." Then I turned and walked away.

PART ELEVEN

"OPEN ARMS AND SLOBBERY KISSES"

Children Loving

Hello, God. This is Laura. May I speak to Jesus? Oh, Jesus is in the garden. Can You get Him? I'll wait.

Oh, hi, Jesus! How are the disciples? I miss You, too. I love You. I'll let You go. Bye Jesus. Tell God bye.

—LAURA, age three, phoning heaven

Thank You for dying on the cross. You are the best friend in the world. I love You.

—ELIZABETH, age seven

To love and be loved…is every kid's dream.

—GRACE, age six, finishing the sentence her
grandmother started

I never knew the depths of love until I looked into the eyes of my newborn child.

—WAYNE HOLMES, age fifty-three (but still a kid
at heart)

I think the closest I ever come to seeing pure love is through the lives of children. I remember the joy I felt when my children were very young, and they were so glad to see me that they'd throw their arms around me, hold and squeeze me, and then plant a big kiss right on my lips. The words "I love you, Daddy" were a nice added touch, but their actions had already demonstrated what was in their hearts.

I'm embarrassed to admit this, but somewhere along the way I learned to love conditionally. I learned to give love only if I was certain to get love. I learned to withhold affection if I wasn't certain it would be accepted and given back in equal portion.

Not kids. To borrow an expression from my friend Mike Brewer, kids love with "open arms and slobbery kisses." I'm not so sure people would appreciate the slobbery kisses coming from an adult, but I'm trying to love once more with open arms.

Let us return to the simple faith of a child who believes in love and isn't afraid to give it freely.

—*Wayne*

COMMUNION

Eugene H. Peterson

from *Living the Message*

When my daughter, Karen, was young, I often took her with me when I visited nursing homes. She was better than a Bible. The elderly in these homes brightened immediately when she entered the room, delighted in her smile, and asked her questions. They touched her skin, stroked her hair. On one such visit we were with Mrs. Herr, who was in an advanced state of dementia. Talkative, she directed all her talk to Karen. She told her a story, an anecdote out of her own childhood that Karen's presence must have triggered, and when she completed it, she immediately repeated it word for word, and then again and again and again. After twenty minutes or so of this, I became anxious lest Karen become uncomfortable and confused about what was going on. I interrupted the flow of talk, anointed the woman with oil, laid hands on her, and prayed. In the car and driving home, I commended Karen for her patience and attentiveness. She had listened to this repeated story without showing any signs of restlessness or boredom. I said, "Karen, Mrs. Herr's mind is not working the way ours are." And Karen said, "Oh, I knew that, Daddy; she wasn't trying to tell us any *thing*. She was telling us who she *is*."

Nine years old, and she knew the difference, knew that Mrs. Herr was using words not for communication but for communion. It is a difference that our culture as a whole pays little attention to but that pastors must pay attention to. Our primary task, the pastor's primary task, is not communication but communion.

> Words kill, words give life;
>> they're either poison or fruit—you choose. (Proverbs 18:21)

◄o►◄o►

Editor's Note: Although there is no prayer offered in this story, I chose it because a prayer principle is involved here. I'm embarrassed to tell you how many times I've come to God and presented the same petitions over and over. Just as Karen understood that Mrs. Herr wasn't trying to communicate but to commune, so my heavenly Father understands that what we often do in prayer is more than offer words. We come offering to let Him know who we are, and we come to commune with Him in anticipation of getting to know who He is.

God listens patiently, never interrupting us, for He is thrilled to have us come into His presence.

TELLING THE TRUTH

Sheila Walsh

from *Living Fearlessly*

B arry, Christian, and I always travel together. We've done so ever since Christian was six weeks old. But in the fall of 1999, I took a three-day trip without them. We were at the end of our hectic year, and we were all tired and a bit under the weather. We had gotten back from a conference in Charlotte, North Carolina, on a Sunday night, and I was scheduled to leave for Dallas at 6:00 the next morning. Barry and I talked about whether I should break our custom and go by myself. I knew I'd be busy each day as we filmed the opening video for "Women of Faith 2000." It seemed to make more sense for everyone else to rest. My father-in-law, William, lives with us, so I felt comfortable that my boy would be fine with Daddy and Papa to take care of him.

While I was gone, I talked to Christian on the phone every morning and every evening, and sometimes at lunch as well. I had hidden three presents in different parts of the house, and each day I would tell him where to find a new one. He seemed to be doing well.

Then I got home. He was a little quiet. He told me what he had been doing, but I sensed, as mothers often do, that something was a bit off. That night as I was rocking him, I asked him if he was all right. He said he was just fine. I said to him, "You know, darling, sometimes you might be angry with Mommy or Daddy, and that's all right. You can tell us."

He looked at me for a moment and then gave me his little sign that he wanted to whisper something in my ear. I bent down.

"Mommy, I'm angry with you," he whispered. "You left me."

I hugged him and told him I was sorry. I rocked him and held him tight, thanking God that children are honest enough to let us into their pain so that moms and dads can share it. When Christian fell asleep that night, I thought about what he had done and how hard it would have been for me. I don't like to let people know they've hurt me. I don't like to make myself that vulnerable. I hate being *needy*, and yet I am. We all are.

One of the biggest challenges in my marriage is to let Barry into my disappointments. I expect him just to get it—which is, of course, unfair and unrealistic. Perhaps it's not so different with God. I'm learning to invite God into all my questions about him. I'm learning to crawl right up into the Father's lap and tell him that I'm angry, I'm afraid, I'm sad. We are invited to do that, you know. He will be there. He will hold us. Rather than diminishing our relationship with him, there will be a depth of intimacy born out of honesty, out of bringing our unseen self, our secret self, so full of questions and fears, to him.

◄○►◄○►

Editor's Note: Just as Sheila invited her son to confide anything and everything, so God invites His children to confide in Him, to whisper in His ear. We may take our emotions, even our anger, and share them with Him in prayer. He loves us unreservedly. When we release our emotions to Him, our love for Him and intimacy with Him increase too.

THE GOD WHO GIVES BACK

Bruce Wilkinson

from *A Life God Rewards*

> Do not lay up for yourselves treasures on earth, where
> moth and rust destroy and where thieves break in and
> steal; but lay up for yourselves treasures in heaven,
> where neither moth nor rust destroys and where
> thieves do not break in and steal.
> —JESUS, in Matthew 6:19-20

I was taking a coffee break during a family conference in Kentucky when Will walked up and stood beside my chair. He was about nine. He asked if I wanted to donate to a missions project.

"What would you use my money for?" I asked.

Will held out a radio. "This radio runs by sun power," he said proudly. "It's for people who live in the jungles. People can listen to this radio to learn things and hear about Jesus."

I decided on the spot to make Will an offer. "Tell you what," I said, "I'll give to your project, but I have a rule that says you have to give money first." On one of his donation cards, I wrote out my proposal:

Will,
If you give one to five dollars,
   I'll give double what you give.

If you give six to ten dollars,

   I'll give triple what you give.

If you give eleven to twenty dollars,

   I'll give four times what you give.

I signed my name and Will read the card. By the time he was finished, his eyes were as big as saucers. Then suddenly his face fell, and he stared at the floor.

"Don't you like my idea?" I asked.

"Yeah," he said, shuffling his feet.

"Well, what are you going to do?"

"Nothing."

"Nothing?"

"I can't," he said. "I already gave everything I had."

I felt a pang in my heart. "You mean you put all your money in your own fund drive?" I asked.

He nodded.

"So you can't buy any more snacks for the rest of the conference?"

He nodded again.

At that moment, I knew what I needed to do. "Actually, Will," I began, "I also have a rule that if you give everything you have, I will give everything I have, too."

As it happened, I'd just been to a bank to withdraw a considerable amount of cash for my trip. I reached under the table for my briefcase, pulled out a bank envelope of bills, and handed it to Will.

I'm not sure who was more surprised—Will or me. Now both of us had eyes as big as saucers, but we were both grinning happily.

◄O►◄O►

Editor's Note: Will's willingness to give everything he had—even without the prospect of receiving anything in return—demonstrates the simple faith of children. When children pray and ask God to come into their lives, they do it without bargaining. They simply give God everything— everything they own and every bit of who they are. Too often adults want to bargain with God. "I'll give you these areas of my life, but I want to hold on to this section for a while." Or we may hope for the system of multiplying returns. We're willing to give, but only in hopes that God will multiply our gift back to us.

What a beautiful example little nine-year-old Will sets. Give it all to God. Let's give all of who we are to God. When we do, He will give all of who He is back to us.

ANNIE'S PRAYER

Jean Davis

I 'll call her Annie. She is now six years old. I met her at a three-day women's conference at our church. The second night of the conference, we returned as a group from supper at a local restaurant to find a man with two young children, a girl and a boy, sitting in the back of the sanctuary.

Someone could have said, "This is a women's conference, you know, and none of you are women, so you need to leave." Maybe it was the duffel bag and the backpack that prevented anyone from asking the man to leave. Maybe it was the small boy's timidity that allowed us all to be extremely kind. Surely it was the love of Jesus.

Several women talked to the man before the service started. They learned that the girl's mother was in prison in another state, and the man had been given custody of the children until her release. They had just come to town to be with him. The boy was his biological child, and even though the girl, Annie, wasn't, she still considered him to be her dad.

One woman later reported that when she spoke to the man and the children about Jesus at the beginning of the meeting, Annie asked, "Who's Jesus?"

Though she and her brother may have been unfamiliar with the reason for our gathering, as the service began, the children participated with us in praise and worship. The boy seemed happy to sit in the back row by his dad and beat on a drum. Annie, however, moved up front with the women. What they did, she did with much enthusiasm. When they rejoiced, she rejoiced and lifted her hands in praise. As they sang, she sang, though she didn't know the words. When they prayed, Annie was at the altar on her knees.

When some of the women played musical instruments, Annie took a tambourine to make a joyful noise. We brandished pompoms in celebration as we praised Him, and Annie chose blue ones. Through it all she kept turning to smile at me. I was totally taken in by the girl. The sparkle, life, and laughter in her eyes made me think of Jesus. I loved her immediately. At the end of the service, several women ministered to her father and prayed for him. Then someone led Annie to the Lord. Annie, child of God, March 14, 2003, 10:02 p.m. Five years old.

The next morning, Saturday, the man came back with his children for the continental breakfast before the meeting started. There was something about Annie's eyes that drew me to her. I felt an urgency to teach her everything I knew.

"God loves you so much. You make Him happy," I said as I picked Annie up to hug her. "You are special to Him. He will never leave you. Every day you can talk to God. You can talk to Him about anything."

I took her with me around the room before the meeting began. "We can pray for others. We can bless them. If they are sick, we can lay hands on them, and God promises He will make them well." We approached every woman in the room and spoke a short blessing over them. As I laid my hands on each woman, Annie's little hands rested on each person right beside mine.

"God, thank You for Mary, and give her peace… God, give Evelyn the desires of her heart… Father, give Ruby a happy heart… God, make Becka well…"

Finally, we approached Annie's dad. "Every day, you can be your dad's helper by praying for him," I said. "Wherever you are, you can pray for him. God hears your prayers, and your prayers make a difference." Then Annie and I prayed for her dad.

After the service started, Annie pointed to the microphone at the podium and told me, "I want to go up there. Will you go with me? I want to talk on that thing." I followed her up to the platform. Someone else was using the microphone to lead us in worship, so we waited.

We waited and waited. When no one acknowledged us, I got down on one knee to ask Annie what she wanted to say. "I want to say, 'Jesus, make all the mean people happy and all the sick people well.'" After a while, Annie left the platform and sat down. I followed. Her dad and brother left the church with her before I had a chance to talk to her again. Annie never got to share her prayer.

On Sunday morning after the conference, a young mother of two shared that sometimes she felt mean in dealing with her children. I shared Annie's prayer with her. "Jesus, make all the mean people happy and all the sick people well." I don't really think this mom had an ounce of mean-ness in her, but I do think she was well acquainted with mommy stress. We all have stress of some kind. We all need prayer.

A few weeks after the women's conference, I saw Annie's dad again, but the children weren't with him.

"How's Annie?" I asked. He told me the children had been taken out of his care and placed in a foster home. He said the day the authorities came after the children, he sat in the cab of his pickup with the children, and someone had to physically pry Annie and her brother out of his arms. She was crying, clinging to him, pleading with the man she considered her dad.

It has been a year since I've seen this child, but I've thought about her many times. I pray for her now as her seventh birthday approaches. Some-times I weep for her. I long to see her again, to hold her close to my heart, to comfort her, to comfort myself with her presence. Whenever I want to pray, *God, fry all the mean people,* I know He sent Annie to teach me how to pray the simple prayer of a child.

So I yield. *God, change the hearts of all the mean people so they can be happy, and make all the wounded people whole. Amen.*

LITTLE SIGNS OF LOVE

Sharon Hinck

T he organ swelled in a Thanksgiving hymn. Joel, my eighteen-month-old son, squirmed in the pew beside me and clutched his teddy bear. The bear's tummy sported a heart embroidered with the words "God Loves You." As I smiled into Joel's blue eyes, I felt my cold discouragement thaw for a moment.

My gaze rested on the bear's message. "God Loves You." I had always known it. I grew up believing it. But today the words sounded hollow.

As the service began I tried to pinpoint the source of my depression. My husband, Ted, and I had moved cross-country to go back to school. Both of us were taking classes and working. Our frantic schedules left little time for each other or for fellowship with other Christians. We felt isolated so far away from family and friends. Financial pressures added to my stress.

The pastor rose to begin the sermon. I patted my growing abdomen and thought of the new baby on the way. Familiar doubts and fears invaded my mind. How would we manage? I struggled to concentrate on the sermon, but worries drowned out the words. Why did everything have to be so hard?

The church service finally ended, and Joel scampered into the hall while Ted and I gathered our things. When we caught up with our son, he no longer had his teddy bear. Because "God Loves You Bear" was one of his favorite toys, we searched the church. Eventually we had to give up. The bear had vanished.

As we settled into our rusty old Datsun, I mumbled dryly, "Well, that's appropriate."

"What is?" Ted asked.

"Losing 'God Loves You Bear.' That's what I feel like I've been losing—God's love."

It was true. Of all the pressures and anxieties that troubled me, the most frightening was the sense of losing touch with God. It was no longer easy to believe He really loved me.

The next week I stopped at church to search again for Joel's "God Loves You Bear." The pastor helped me look, but neither of us located it. Someone must have found it and taken it home. I walked out to the parking lot, discouraged.

As I drove home, a strange thought stirred in my mind: *Pray for the teddy bear.*

I laughed. God didn't seem to be involving Himself in the big problems Ted and I were facing. Why would He care about a lost teddy bear?

Pray for the bear, the thought insisted.

Ridiculous! It was the kind of thing I would have prayed about when I was a young Christian and faith came easy. Back then little miracles were daily occurrences. But those days seemed long ago.

Pray for the bear.

Crazy. We had searched everywhere. There was no way it would ever turn up again.

Pray for the bear.

"All right!" I blurted out loud. Joel's wide eyes watched me from his car seat.

I managed a reassuring smile. "I think we're supposed to pray for your bear."

Joel nodded. "Okay. I pray." He lifted his folded hands with enthusiasm. "My bear. Give me back. Thank You, Jesus-loves-me."

I cleared my throat. "Please find Joel's teddy bear."

Silently my prayer continued. *Lord, if You still do love me, please show me. Give me a sign. I know You don't need to prove Yourself to me, but I've been so discouraged. Please reassure me. Please find the bear—for both of us.* Tears ran down my face. That was one of the most heartfelt prayers I'd offered in a long time.

"Amen." Joel's voice piped up.

I glanced at him, and he gave me a chubby, confident smile.

Homework, time with our busy boy, and Christmas preparations filled the following weeks. Our family struggled, quarreled, muddled along, and survived.

Christmas Eve arrived in a quiet, unassuming way. Again Ted and I sat in the back church pew, watching Joel squirm. Once again I felt unlovable and far from God. I had forgotten my secret, impassioned plea to God for a sign.

The organist had begun the prelude when I felt a tap on my shoulder. Our pastor said, "I have something for you. I'll be right back."

A moment later he returned—to hand Joel the stuffed bear with "God Loves You" across its tummy. Shock spiraled up my spine. "It was outside my office door when I came in to work," the pastor said. "Someone must have found it."

He hurried away for the service. Familiar Christmas music drifted around us. The altar candles blurred as tears filled my eyes. My awareness sharpened when Ted's hand touched mine as he moved closer to share the hymnal. Baby-on-the-way stirred inside me. Joel happily hugged his bear, content in an answered prayer that he had never doubted. His faith life wasn't scuffed up with the confusions of life like mine was. His prayer life was simple: Tell God the problem and watch for Him to take care of things.

The signs were all around me. The Son, whose arrival we were celebrating, affirmed it. The little bear proclaimed it. Once again my heart believed it: "God Loves You."

A Mark of Grace

H. Michael Brewer

M ark blew into our congregation like Pentecost, with noisy commotion, wildfire energy, and a spirit of irresistible joy. How could one eight-year-old boy unsettle an entire congregation with nearly one hundred years of unruffled tradition? Mark had a knack.

For instance, during the children's sermon, Mark explored the room, sniffing flowers, peeking under the shiny coverings on the Communion plates, testing the water in the baptismal font. At a solemn moment in the service, Mark might wander up front and climb into the arms of the liturgist. While others sat in Calvinistic solemnity, Mark scooted around beneath the pews studying feet and tugging shoelaces.

Mark was born with an extremely rare genetic condition that arrested his mental development. He would never be able to read or write, and his speech consisted of barely understandable words in broken phrases. Nevertheless, it would not be accurate to say that Mark suffered from a disability. Mark was not a sufferer, but a rejoicer. Mark reveled in life.

In Mark's world there were no strangers, only friends at the mall, on the bus, in the street. In his view, every empty lap was an invitation to become better acquainted. In fact, he delighted in all living creatures. An ant was an antennae-waving marvel. A honeybee was astonishing; a tropical fish more wondrous than an angel. Unlike most of us, Mark never became jaded or indifferent to everyday miracles.

Initially, our congregation displayed some uneasiness with Mark. After all, he was different, and the fear of those who are different is deeply ingrained in us. What if Mark became disruptive? What if he had needs we couldn't meet?

Then, without warning, God intervened.

One Sunday morning at the conclusion of the children's sermon, the pastor said, "Let's pray." Children and adults obediently bowed their heads, waiting for the polished, professional prayer from the lips of the seminary-trained minister, but Mark suddenly changed the rules. Before the pastor could utter another word, Mark began to pray aloud in a clear voice that carried to every corner of the room.

"Dear Jesus," Mark began. There followed a singsong stream of mostly unintelligible words. Here and there we could pick out the names of animals, as Mark gave thanks—or interceded—for elephants, tigers, and lobsters. After a few minutes Mark drew a deep breath and concluded with "A-a-a-a-a-a-men!"

After Mark had finished, the congregation sat hushed. Some worshipers were smiling broadly; others wept openly. A few were doing both. Unexpectedly, our predictable worship service had stumbled onto holy ground, and we savored the moment.

That's when we finally realized that Mark wasn't a distraction; he was a gift. Mark's presence wasn't a challenge, but a grace. He had dropped in on us not so that we could teach him but so that we could learn from him—about gifts, about loving God from the heart, about open arms and slobbery kisses, about the wonders wrapped in the humblest person and the blessings hidden within each and every child of God.

For the next few weeks, Mark prayed after each children's sermon. Then, one Sunday, he stopped abruptly and returned the prayer to the minister. We never knew why. Probably Mark decided that he'd made his point.

And he was right!

Author Profiles

Whispering in God's Ear is a collection of previously published and original stories. The following author profiles have been included only for the authors who wrote original material for this book. I hope you will take the time to read about these special people and check out some of their other published works.

MICHELLE MEDLOCK ADAMS has earned first-place awards from the Associated Press, the Hoosier State Press Association, and the Society of Professional Journalists. Michelle has published thousands of articles in prestigious publications such as *Writer's Digest* and *Today's Christian Woman*. She is also the author of fifteen books, including her award-winning picture book *Conversations on the Ark*. Learn more about Michelle at *www.michellemedlockadams.com*.

DIANA J. BAKER is married to Pastor Larry H. Baker. She is a mother, grandmother, teacher, freelance writer, pianist, and songwriter. Diana has coauthored one book, and her stories and articles have appeared in Focus on the Family publications and other magazines, newsletters, and anthologies.

PATRICK BORDERS is a freelance writer living near Atlanta, Georgia. He has published several times in *Guideposts* and *In Touch* magazines and in publications such as *HomeLife, The Upper Room,* and *The Christian Communicator*. His stories have also appeared in *The Heart of a Mother* and *The Heart of a Teacher*.

LANITA BRADLEY BOYD, a freelance writer in Fort Thomas, Kentucky, draws from years of experience in teaching, church ministry, and family life in her writing.

She has stories in *The Heart of a Mother* and *The Heart of a Teacher* as well as other anthologies. She can be reached at *lanitaboyd@insightbb.com.*

H. MICHAEL BREWER is a full-time Presbyterian pastor and part-time writer. His most recent publications are *Gotta Have God,* a devotional book for middle-school boys, and *Who Needs a Superhero?* an exploration of Christian theology based on comic-book superheroes. In his spare time he reads, gardens, and kayaks.

JOY BROWN speaks at conferences, seminars, and retreats through the ministry Words of Joy. Joy is a member of the popular women's ministry team Women by Design and has been a speaker/trainer with the nationally known Building Strong Families Foundation. Joy and her husband, Wayne, lead local, state, and national marriage-enrichment retreats.

PAT BUTLER lives and works as a missionary in northern France, where she exercises her faith and writing skills while enjoying French pastries! A native New Yorker, Pat began writing as a child. Although Pat is single, her extended family— French and American—provides an endless source for stories and poems.

PHIL CALLAWAY, editor of *Servant* magazine, is also a popular speaker and the award-winning author of a dozen books, including *Growing Up on the Edge of the World, Making Life Rich Without Any Money,* and *Who Put the Skunk in the Trunk?* He lives in Alberta, Canada, with his high-school sweetheart and their three teenagers.

BRENDA R. COATS and her husband, Shaun, were married in the fall of 1989 in beautiful Ouray, Colorado. Today they reside in Longmont, Colorado, with their three children Ashlee, Jessica, and Andrew. In addition to writing, Brenda enjoys playing the piano, knitting, crocheting, and watching professional football.

LAURIE BARKER COPELAND is a speaker, humorist, actress, and coauthor of *The Groovy Chick Road Trip to Peace*. She lives in Florida with her husband, John, and their daughter, Kailey, who is a constant source of material for Laurie's stories. Find out more about Laurie at *www.lauriecopeland.com*.

JEAN DAVIS has published devotionals for teens and adults and is currently working on a second young-adult novel. She is a member of the Society of Children's Book Writers and Illustrators and lives in Clarksville, Delaware, with her husband.

BARB EIMER is a wife and mother of six and lives in Fort Wayne, Indiana. Her articles have appeared in various magazines including *Pregnancy, MOMSense,* and *The Charlotte Parent*. She's currently writing a parenting book with the working title *Pearls of Wisdom in a Sea of Muck*. You can contact her at *www.barbeimer.com*.

BARBARA EUBANKS, from Boaz, Alabama, is a freelance writer, teacher, minister's wife, mother of three sons, and grandmother of eight. Drawing from these significant roles and people, she has written a devotional book titled *Humorous Happenings in Holy Places*. She has edited and compiled NIE Workshop '89 published by the *Gadsden Times* and has also written articles for magazines and newspapers.

SUSANNA FLORY is a freelance writer residing in Castro Valley, California, with her husband and two children. Ethan is now a teenager. He still prays.

JEAN HALL lives with her husband, Jerry, and mother, Aliene, near Charlotte, North Carolina. She holds an MA in Educational Leadership and has been an educator for more than twenty-eight years. Jean loves the Lord, life, her family, children, gardening, reading, and writing.

EMILY SUE HARVEY'S upbeat stories appear in women's magazines, including *Compassionate Friends, Chocolate for Women, Chicken Soup,* and *Eulogy to Joy.* Her novel *God Only Knows* is represented by the Peter Miller NY Agency. Her most recent project is *Sunny Flavors,* a fictional mill-hill novel of love, loss, family, and forgiveness. You may contact Emily at *EmilySue1@aol.com.*

KELLY HAYES is a full-time mom with a passion for encouraging mothers through the Scriptures. Her devotionals and articles have appeared in *The Secret Place,* Vocational Biographies, and *The Proverbs 31 Woman.* She makes her home in New Freedom, Pennsylvania, with husband, Michael, and their two children.

ANITA HIGMAN is an award-winning author and has published eighteen books for children and adults. Anita has won two awards for her contributions to literacy, has served on the board of directors of Literacy Advance of Houston, and has helped raise thousands of dollars for literacy with her book, *I Can Be Anything!* For more information about Anita Higman and her books, visit her Web site at *www.anitahigman.com.*

DOROTHY HILL is an educator and a former foster parent. When she is not writing, she can be found enjoying her grandchildren (and their parents, of course). She can be reached at *missisip@dixie-net.com.*

SHARON HINCK is an author, wife, and mother of four. Sharon also has an MA in communication from Regent University. While serving as artistic director of a Christian-arts ministry, she went on several short-term missions to Hong Kong. Her family accompanied her on one trip—and Joel was able to bring along a few stuffed animals. Joel is now twenty-one and majoring in music composition in college. He still owns "God Loves You Bear." For information on recent writing projects, visit *www.SharonHinck.com.*

KAREN TENNEY HITCHCOCK is a wife and mother, a women's Bible-study teacher, and a freelance writer. When not watching her children's sporting events, she is an avid reader and sometime gardener. She makes her home in Cincinnati, Ohio.

LINDA KNIGHT is a freelance writer currently writing for *Woman's World* magazine, Miss Charity's Diner (Faithville Gospelcast Productions for kids' television), SPS Studios, Abbey Press, and others. She's also the author of more than three thousand greeting-card verses as well as articles, devotionals, and poems. Linda resides in Woodslee, Ontario, with her husband, Steve.

KATHRYN LAY is a writer, wife, and mom living in Texas. You can learn more about her new children's novel *Crown Me!* as well as her speaking, published writing, and writing classes at *www.kathrynlay.com,* or e-mail her at rlay15@aol.com.

MARILYN MARTYN MCAULEY, author and inspirational speaker, lives in the Pacific Northwest with her husband, Dan, who still teaches. They are proud parents, grandparents, and great-grandparents. They enjoy serving the Lord by mentoring troubled marriages, loving their neighbors, and volunteering in their church.

JANET LYNN MITCHELL is a wife, mother, author, and inspirational speaker. She's authored numerous stories and articles and is the coauthor of *A Special Kind of Love: For Those Who Love Children with Special Needs.* For more information visit *www.JanetLynnMitchell.com.*

PEGGY MORRIS is a gifted writer, pastor's wife, and mother of two sons and a daughter-in-love. She has written for such publications as *Woman's World, Marriage Partnership,* and *War Cry.* She also enjoys writing greeting cards for DaySpring and Christian Inspirations. Her heart is overjoyed knowing her now-grown sons love spending time with God in prayer.

CECIL (CEC) MURPHEY has written, cowritten, or ghostwritten more than one hundred books, including *Gifted Hands, Committed but Flawed,* and *When Someone You Love Has Alzheimer's.*

DONITA K. PAUL is a retired teacher and award-winning author of Christian romance. Her latest book is *DragonSpell,* a Christian allegory in fantasy novel form. She lives in a studio in her married daughter's basement and does all the usual grandma things with her grandsons—reading books, finger painting, and, after lunch, taking the scraps out in the backyard to feed dragons.

LOIS PECCE and her husband live in Centerville, Ohio. Lois is active in the Dayton Christian Scribes writer's group and enjoys writing about life in general. She especially delights in the fresh insights of children. Through the years she's published more than two hundred articles, stories, and poems.

DIANE H. PITTS resides on the Gulf Coast with her husband and three boys. When she is not drinking tea with "The Ward Road Women" and writing about their escapades, Diane works as a physical therapist, troubleshoots for missionaries, and loses herself in music. Visit her at *http://www.dianehpitts.com.*

MARTHA ROGERS is a retired teacher, mother, grandmother, and freelance writer. She has written eight Bible studies, numerous devotionals and articles for compilations, and several magazine articles. Martha is also the director of Texas Christian Writer's Conference and president of the State Board of Inspirational Writers Alive! writing groups of Texas.

STACY ROTHENBERGER is a speech and language therapist, freelance author, and mother of five children. Sharing all of her mistakes and trials in her own marriage and parenting endeavors was something she never considered doing. But God is teaching her through the daily struggles and victories in her Christian walk the importance of never saying never.

JENNIFER A. SCHUCHMANN is a writer and speaker who is active in her Atlanta-area church where she first heard Emma's story. She has written on business, church, and arts-management topics and teaches an adult Bible class. Her coteacher became her coauthor for her latest book, *Your Unforgettable Life: Only You Can Choose the Legacy You Leave* (Beacon Hill Press, summer 2005). Writing this book has helped Jennifer hear God in new ways. You can learn more about her at *www.jenniferschuchmann.com*.

LYNN SCHWANDER freelances for Pacific Northwest newspapers. She loves writing for children, kids'-ministry workers, and a Japanese University English department. She's presently working on a novel for preteens. On the weekends, when not cleaning the hamster cage, Lynn and her husband enjoy watching their two children play soccer.

JANET SKETCHLEY is a Canadian writer of inspirational articles and fiction. She and her husband, Russell, now have three boys: Adam, Andrew, and Matthew. Andrew's doily days are long past, but Janet has saved a few remnants as keepsakes.

PATRICIA STEBELTON lives in Chelsea, Michigan. She enjoys writing, freelance art work, family camping, and teaching Bible at Florida's Juvenile Detention Center during the winter. Patricia and her husband find great joy in knowing that their

three children are happily married and their grandchildren are being taught
God's love and principles.

PATTY STUMP is a popular speaker at women's retreats and special events, a contributing writer to eighteen books, a workshop leader, and a substitute women's
Bible-study leader at the Billy Graham Training Center at The Cove in Asheville,
North Carolina. Patty resides in Montreat, North Carolina, with her husband
and two children.

ELIZABETH M. THOMPSON is a freelance writer living in Elk Grove, California.
She is a passionate Bible student and enjoys using her gifts to kindle a love of
God's Word in others. Her articles have appeared in Focus on the Family's *Citi-
zen* magazine, *On the Town,* and *Writer's Block.* Her family includes husband,
Michael, and children Gabrielle, Nathaniel, and Julia.

HEIDI VANDERSLIKKE lives on a farm in rural Ontario, Canada, with her husband, Jack, and their three children. She writes devotional material and family-
life articles and is a columnist for the *Christian Courier.*

C. ELLEN WATTS writes regularly for Christian and inspirational markets. This
homemaker and author of five books—two more in progress—is mom to five,
grandmother to sixteen, and a great-grandmother. She enjoys traveling with her
husband, mentoring young mothers and fledgling writers, and teaching writing
classes.

LISA EBLEN WIENER has written articles for newsletters about and for people who
use wheelchairs. She has also written curriculum for children's groups known as
"Winners on Wheels." She's been published in *The Christian Communicator,*

Moody Magazine, The Upper Room, and *Alliance Life.* She also serves as the director for Christian Writers' Group—*http://ChristianWritersGroup.org.*

JoAnn Reno Wray lives in Broken Arrow, Oklahoma, and has been married thirty-five years to Roger. Writing for more than thirty years, she has been published in more than one thousand online and print publications. She also teaches and speaks regularly. You can learn more about JoAnn, her business EpistleWorks Creations, and her magazine *Melody of the Heart* at *http://epistleworks.com.*

Jeanne Zornes is a widely published, award-winning author and speaker who focuses on God's encouragement and encouraging others. Her books include *When I Felt Like Ragweed, God Saw a Rose: The Power of Encouragement.* She and her husband live in Wenatchee, Washington, and have two young-adult children. Learn more about her at *www.classervices.com.*

CREDITS AND PERMISSIONS

E very effort was made to secure proper permission and acknowledgment for each story in this work. If you discover an error, please accept my apologies and contact WaterBrook Press at 2375 Telstar Drive, Suite 160, Colorado Springs, Colorado, 80920, so that corrections can be made in future editions.

Permission to reprint any of the stories from this work must be obtained from the original source. Acknowledgments are listed by story title in the order in which they appear in the book. Heartfelt thanks to all the authors and publishers for generously allowing their work to be included in this collection.

PART ONE: "PLEASE LET ME SEE A FROG"

"Five Is Not Too Young" by Corrie ten Boom. Reprinted from *In My Father's House* by Corrie ten Boom. Copyright © 1976 by Corrie ten Boom and Carole C. Carlson. Used by permission of Fleming H. Revell Company, a division of Baker Publishing Group, and Hodder and Stoughton Limited. All rights reserved.

"Plum Purple City Lights" by Janet Lynn Mitchell. Copyright © 2004. Used by permission. All rights reserved. A version of this story appeared in *A Special Kind of Love: For Those Who Love Children with Special Needs* by Susan Titus Osborn and Janet Lynn Mitchell. Copyright © 2004 by Janet Lynn Mitchell. Used by permission of Broadman and Holman. All rights reserved.

"A Mother's Day Prayer" by Stacy Rothenberger. Copyright © 2004. Used by permission. All rights reserved.

"A Son's Prayer" by Martha Rogers. Copyright © 2004. Used by permission. All rights reserved.

"Nikes and Mustard Seeds" by Susanna Flory. Copyright © 2004. Used by permission. All rights reserved.

"I Lift Up My Eyes to the Hills" by Jeanne Zornes. Copyright © 2004. Used by permission. All rights reserved.

"A Simple Prayer" by Kathryn Lay. Copyright © 2004. Used by permission. All rights reserved.

PART TWO: "HELP ME NOT LIKE MY ANIMALS"

"Shirley's Story" by Gloria Gaither and Shirley Dobson. Reprinted by permission. *Let's Make a Memory* by Gloria Gaither and Shirley Dobson, copyright © 1983, 1994, W Publishing, Nashville, Tennessee. All rights reserved.

"Faith in God's Living Word" by Sally Clarkson. Reprinted from *The Ministry of Motherhood.* Copyright © 2004 by Sally Clarkson. Used by permission of WaterBrook Press, Colorado Springs, CO. All rights reserved.

"Smokin' Joe" by Barb Eimer. Copyright © 2004. Used by permission. All rights reserved.

"A Little Boy's Prayer" by Janet Sketchley. Copyright © 2004. Used by permission. All rights reserved.

"Listening Prayers" by Jennifer A. Schuchmann. Copyright © 2004. Used by permission. All rights reserved.

"Of Teddy Bears and Missionaries" by Sharon Hinck. Copyright © 2004. Used by permission. All rights reserved.

PART THREE: "WHEN I GROW UP"

PART FOUR: "I FOUND IT"

PART FIVE: "I HAVE HEARD HIS VOICE"

Part Six: "Dear Jesus, We Need a Daddy"

"Bibles, Baptism, Certificates, and Other Signs of Church Life" by Beth
    Moore. Reprinted from *Feathers from My Nest: A Mother's Reflections* by
    Beth Moore. Copyright © 2001 by Beth Moore. Reprinted and used
    by permission of LifeWay Christian Resources of the Southern Baptist
    Convention, Nashville, Tennessee.

"Innocent Petitions" by Robin Jones Gunn. Reprinted from *Mothering by
    Heart,* copyright © 1996, 2002 by Robin Jones Gunn. Used by permis-
    sion of Multnomah Publishers Inc.

"The Problem" by Gigi Graham. Originally appeared in *Weatherproof Your
    Heart,* copyright © 1991. Published by Fleming H. Revell. Used by
    permission of Gigi Graham. All rights reserved.

"Wanted: A Friend" by Lynn Schwander. Copyright © 2004. Used by permis-
    sion. All rights reserved.

" 'We Need a Daddy' " by Marilyn Martyn McAuley. Copyright © 2004. Used
    by permission. All rights reserved.

"Kelsey's Prayer" by Lanita Bradley Boyd. Copyright © 2004. Used by permis-
    sion. All rights reserved.

"Trey's Prayer" by Dorothy Hill. Copyright © 2004. Used by permission. All
    rights reserved.

Part Seven: "Do I Haf to Tell You What I Done?"

"Disowned Desire" by John Eldredge. Reprinted by permission. *The Journey
    of Desire* by John Eldredge, copyright © 2000, W Publishing, Nashville,
    Tennessee. All rights reserved.

PART EIGHT: "WOULD YOU PLEASE HEAL MY GRANDPA?"

Part Nine: "Wow, God!"

" 'Pão, Senhor?' " by Max Lucado. Reprinted by permission. *No Wonder They Call Him the Savior* by Max Lucado, copyright © 1995, W Publishing, Nashville, Tennessee. All rights reserved.

"Bedtime Rituals" by Lori Borgman. Reprinted from *Pass the Faith, Please.* Copyright © 2004 by Lori Borgman. Used by permission of WaterBrook Press, Colorado Springs, Colorado. All rights reserved.

"Disabled Dreams" by Tamara Boggs. Taken from *Children Are a Blessing from the Lord* © 2001 by Tamara Boggs. Published by Kregel Publications, Grand Rapids, MI. Used by permission of the publisher. All rights reserved.

"The Day the Sandman Came" by Gigi Graham. Originally appeared in *Weatherproof Your Heart,* copyright © 1991. Published by Fleming H. Revell. Used by permission of Gigi Graham. All rights reserved.

"Just Say 'Wow!' " by Barbara Eubanks. Copyright © 2004. Used by permission. All rights reserved.

"A Holy Presence" by Lois Pecce. Copyright © 2004. Used by permission. All rights reserved.

Part Ten: "In the Name of Jesus"

"The Laying On of Hands" by Richard J. Foster. Excerpt of 536 words from pp. 209-10 from *Prayer: Finding the Heart's True Home* by Richard J. Foster. Copyright © 1992 by Richard J. Foster. Reprinted by permission of HarperCollins Publishers, Inc., and William Neill-Hall Ltd. All rights reserved.

" 'It's Okay, Mommy' " by Michelle Medlock Adams. Copyright © 2004. Used by permission. All rights reserved.

"One Child's Prayer" by Patricia Stebelton. Copyright © 2004. Used by
    permission. All rights reserved.

"Simple Faith" by Lisa Eblen Wiener. Copyright © 2004. Used by permission.
    All rights reserved.

"A Prayer of Faith" by Diana J. Baker. Copyright © 2004. Used by permission.
    All rights reserved.

"A Brother's Gift" by Emily Sue Harvey. Copyright © 2004. Used by permis-
    sion. All rights reserved.

PART ELEVEN: "OPEN ARMS AND SLOBBERY KISSES"

"Communion" by Eugene H. Peterson. Reprinted from *Living the Message,*
    copyright © 1996 by Eugene H. Peterson. Published by HarperSanFran-
    cisco, a division of HarperCollins. Used by permission of Eugene H.
    Peterson. All rights reserved.

"Telling the Truth" by Sheila Walsh. Taken from *Living Fearlessly* by Sheila
    Walsh. Copyright © 2001 by Sheila Walsh. Used by permission of The
    Zondervan Corporation.

"The God Who Gives Back" by Bruce Wilkinson. Excerpted from *A Life God
    Rewards* by Bruce Wilkinson © 2002 by Exponential, Inc. Used by per-
    mission of Multnomah Publishers Inc.

"Annie's Prayer" by Jean Davis. Copyright © 2004. Used by permission. All
    rights reserved.

"Little Signs of Love" by Sharon Hinck. Copyright © 2004. Used by permis-
    sion. All rights reserved.

"A Mark of Grace" by H. Michael Brewer. Copyright © 2004. Used by
    permission. All rights reserved.